fine
Gardening

POCKET GARDENS

fine Gardening

POCKET GARDENS

FROM THE EDITORS & CONTRIBUTORS
OF *FINE GARDENING*

The Taunton Press

The Taunton Press
Inspiration for hands-on living®

The Taunton Press, Inc.
63 South Main Street, PO Box 5506
Newtown, CT 06470-5506
e-mail: tp@taunton.com

Editor: Jennifer Renjilian-Morris
Indexer: Jim Curtis
Cover design: Kim Adis
Interior design: Kim Adis, Stacy Wakefield
Layout: Stacy Wakefield
Cover photographer: Brian Vanden Brink

Fine Gardening® is a trademark of The Taunton Press, Inc., registered in the U.S. Patent
and Trademark Office.

The following names/manufacturers appearing in *Fine Gardening Pocket Gardens* are trademarks:
Big Wheels®, Callie® Orange calibrachoa, Havahart®, Lavender Twist™, Little Henry®, Little
Trudy™, Madness™ Red petunia, Oso Easy®, Tiny Tower®, Tropicanna® canna

Library of Congress Cataloging-in-Publication Data
Fine gardening pocket gardens : design ideas for small-space gardening / author: editors &
contributors of Fine gardening.
     p. cm.
  Design ideas for small-space gardening
  Includes index.
  ISBN 978-1-62113-794-8
1. Gardens--Design. 2. Small gardens. I. Fine gardening. II. Title: Design ideas for small-space
gardening.
  SB473. F57 2013
  635--dc23
                    2013037617

Printed in the United States of America
10 9 8 7 6 5 4 3 2 1

ACKNOWLEDGMENTS

Thanks to the many contributors—authors, photographers, illustrators, and editors—to Fine Gardening *magazine. Thanks to the book's editors: Jennifer Renjilian Morris, for all of her hard work putting this book together, and Renee I. Neiger, for overseeing the project.*

CONTENTS

BASICS

EDIBLE GARDENS

DECORATIVE GARDENS

PLANTS FOR SMALL SPACES

INTRODUCTION

IF YOU HAVE EVER SEEN A PLANT SPROUTING FROM A CRACK IN the pavement, you can understand that plants will grow almost anywhere. So you can just forget the idea that you can't have a garden because you don't have enough room. As this book will show you, all you need is a little extra attention to choosing your plants, evaluating your conditions, and designing your space. But in the end, whether you want to grow edibles, ornamentals, or both, plants are plants, so after a little attention to the basics, you will find informative and inspirational chapters that will turn your small space into something special.

Steve Aitken, Editor, Fine Gardening

BASICS

THREE PRIME CHEMICAL ELEMENTS ARE FOUND IN ALL MIXED FERTILIZERS

Nitrogen (N) promotes healthy leaf growth by stimulating the production of chlorophyll (the main chemical involved in photosynthesis—how plants convert sunlight to food).

Phosphorus (P) supports the vigorous development of roots, stems, blossoms, and fruits.

Potassium (K) plays a key role in helping plants digest and manufacture their foods.

FERTILIZING
BASICS

For all gardeners, knowledge of fertilizers and how to apply them effectively is as crucial to vigorous plant growth as knowing a plant's hardiness zones. So in the interest of growing healthy plants, garden designer Sandra Gorry has demystified the why, what, how, and when of applying these multivitamins.

ALL OF THE NUTRIENTS ESSENTIAL TO PLANT GROWTH ARE PRESENT IN THE soil or are floating in the air, so what's the point of fertilizing? The point is that not all plants can access the key nutrients found in the soil or in the air. Each soil type has its own mix of nutritional ingredients, so before considering what fertilizers a plant may require, we need to consider the soil in which a plant is growing. Activities like intensive farming, construction, and traffic can alter soil chemistry and structure, limiting the nutrients that plants can use. In some cases, the nutrients aren't naturally there to begin with or have been leached out over time. For these reasons, we, the diggers of the dirt and keepers of the garden, must replenish, replace, or help release those elements that are beyond the reach of our plants.

When it comes to fertilizing, more does not mean better. It is possible to overfeed your plants. Too much fertilizer can damage and maybe even kill your plants. Before applying any fertilizer, it's a good idea to have your soil tested so you can select the type and formula that suits your plants' needs. In return, our plants will reward us with bigger flowers, bigger leaves, and bigger fruits and vegetables.

WHAT PLANTS NEED

The three essential elements that all plants need are nitrogen, phosphorus, and potassium—or N-P-K, the proportions of which are stated as numbers on the package. For instance, a general-purpose fertilizer labeled 20-20-20 means that each chemical element—N, P, and K—contributes 20 percent by weight to the total formula (the remaining 40 percent is composed of inert materials

Look to the label. The nutrient ratio tells how much N-P-K is in the fertilizer mix.

CHOOSING THE RIGHT TYPE

It comes down to a question of what works best for your site and your time.

GRANULAR APPLICATIONS

Granular fertilizers deliver food to a plant slowly but have the advantage of longevity.

Broadcast application This method, which covers large areas well, is used to apply granular fertilizers to lawns or to new beds before they are planted. The broadcast method can be done with a hand-rotary or drop spreader.

Top-dress application This technique, which provides nutrients to individual plants such as shrubs and perennials, is done by hand with granular fertilizers. Simply apply the fertilizer around the base of the plant, extending to the drip line. For vegetables, place the fertilizer in a strip parallel to the planting row.

WATER-SOLUBLE APPLICATIONS

Water-soluble fertilizers are faster acting but must be applied more frequently.

Base application This method gives plants food while you water. To use water-soluble fertilizers, follow the mixing instructions and water the soil at the plant's base with a watering can or hose attachment. This is good for feeding container plants and vegetables.

Foliar application This approach is similar to base application, but the water is applied to the leaves rather than to the soil. It is useful when plants need to quickly absorb trace elements like iron.

To use a hand-rotary, just crank the handle to release to fertilizer (far left). If you have a lot of ground to cover, a drop spreader comes in handy (left).

Fertilize while you water with a base application (left). If you need to fertilize only a few plants, a top-dress application is a good choice (bottom).

A foliar application delivers nutrients quickly.

and trace elements). The element percentages are offered in varying proportions to suit different fertilizer needs. If you are looking to boost flower production, you want a mix like 15-30-15, which is high in flower-developing phosphorus. If you want to green up your lawn, choose a mix like 25-6-4, which is high in nitrogen. Many fertilizers are formulated for specific plants like roses, bulbs, or vegetables. Be sure to check the label for the N-P-K ratio, as you may be able to use a general fertilizer with close to the same nutrient percentages but at a lower price.

In addition to N-P-K, most fertilizers contain traces of other elements important to plant health. Some trace elements are more important than others, but each nourishes a plant in its own way. The main trace elements in fertilizers are calcium, magnesium, iron, copper, manganese, zinc, molybdenum, boron, and sulfur (you can usually purchase these items individually as well). If any of these elements are lacking, a plant may show characteristic deficiency symptoms. An iron deficiency, for instance, causes chlorosis (yellow leaves with green veins), which is easily corrected with a dose of chelated iron.

There are quite a number of fertilizers available today, both organic (plant and animal derived) and inorganic (chemically derived). While the majority are commercially produced inorganic fertilizers, there are a few options for the organic gardener. Many rely on the old standbys—animal manure and compost—which, although organic and good for soil building, actually contain few nutrients. For flower and fruit development, bonemeal with a high phosphorus count is the organic of choice, while blood meal is a good source of nitrogen.

HOW TO CHOOSE

There are two types of fertilizers available to the home gardener: granular and water soluble. Each type has advantages and disadvantages. Granular fertilizers deliver food to a plant slowly but have the advantage of longevity. Since they must be broken down by water before a plant can use them, granular fertilizers do not leach out of the soil as rapidly as water-soluble types. Water-soluble fertilizers are faster acting but more transient, which means they must be applied more frequently than the granular type.

Both types of fertilizers are effective, so the one you choose depends on whether you want to give your plants a quick but frequent fix or a sluggish but extended feeding. And for those of us gardeners who are oh so very busy (or oh so very lazy), nothing beats time-release granular fertilizers, some of which require only one application every six to nine months.

There are several ways to apply granular and water-soluble fertilizers, but there are a few general guidelines that one should follow when applying them. Avoid applying a fertilizer on windy or rainy days. This can cause it to be misplaced and ineffective. When using a granular fertilizer, always be sure to knock the fertilizer off plant leaves to avoid burn. Never apply a granular fertilizer when the soil is extremely dry, and water it in thoroughly after applying to prevent plant burn.

WHEN TO FERTILIZE

Knowing when to fertilize is as important as using the right fertilizer. If you don't apply the fertilizer at a time when the plant can use it, there's no point in fertilizing. Most perennials, annuals, vegetables, and lawns will reward you handsomely if fed with a balanced granular fertilizer in early spring. Avoid fertilizing before the spring showers, however, or you will be throwing your money away, since the nutrients will simply leach out of the soil. Annuals like to be fed an additional three or four times during the growing season with a high-phosphorus, water-soluble fertilizer, while lawns benefit from a second granular application in early fall.

Trees and shrubs, especially those that flower, also like a dose of a balanced granular fertilizer in the spring and another in the fall. But remember to heed the phrase "late and light" when fertilizing trees and shrubs in autumn. Late fall is also a good time to fertilize bulbs, especially if you are planting them for the first time; a teaspoon of bonemeal added to each bulb hole will generally be sufficient.

Roses have insatiable appetites. To keep them fat and happy, feed them with a soluble fertilizer every seven days during their blooming season. "Weekly, weakly" is the feeding mantra for all roses. One final thought: Feed only well-established plants; fertilizing seeds or tiny seedlings will cause fertilizer burn.

Just remember, these guidelines on feeding are just that—guidelines. Read the package directions before scattering both food and caution to the wind.

THE SCOOP ON FERTILIZER INGREDIENTS

INGREDIENT	WHAT IT DOES	WHERE IT COMES FROM
UREA	Urea supplies nitrogen. When given to plants, urea breaks down into ammonium. This chemical takes less energy for a plant to use than nitrate, the other nitrogen source for plants. But too much ammonium is toxic. Conveniently, ammonium in fertilizer converts naturally into nitrate over the course of days or weeks. Cold weather, however, slows down this conversion. When temperatures dip below 70°F, opt for fertilizers that contain more nitrate (such as potassium nitrate) and less urea or ammonium.	Although the urea in fertilizers is created synthetically, urea does occur naturally in animal urine. The nitrogen in synthetic urea comes from the same place that all synthetic nitrogen comes from: the air. Synthetic nitrogen is made by mixing the nitrogen in air with hydrogen from natural gas at high temperatures and pressures. This process, known as the Haber-Bosch reaction, produces the chemical ammonia, which is the source of almost all synthetic nitrogen.
POTASSIUM CHLORIDE	Potassium chloride consists of potassium and chlorine, both of which are quickly available to plants after the fertilizer is applied. Potassium is vital for growth and photosynthesis, while the chlorine simply makes the potassium water soluble and easier for plants to absorb.	Potassium chloride is a commonly found, natural chemical. It is usually extracted from saltwater, mined from ancient oceans (land that was under seawater eons ago), or produced as a by-product of chemical reactions in a laboratory.
POTASSIUM PHOSPHATE	Potassium phosphate provides plants with phosphorus and more potassium. Plants need phosphorus to produce roots, fruit, and flowers. But too often, fertilizers contain more phosphorus than plants can use, and the excess runs off into waterways.	Although this chemical can occur naturally, it's usually created in a laboratory by combining other potassium- and phosphorus-containing chemicals. Some predict that we'll run out of phosphorus within 100 years because it's being mined so aggressively. To avoid wasting this mineral and polluting the environment, buy fertilizers that are low in phosphorus. A ratio of 4–1–2 is usually plenty.
DISODIUM ZINC EDTA, MANGANESE EDTA, DISODIUM SALT, AND FERRIC SODIUM EDTA	These ingredients are known as chelates, which are chemicals that provide nutrients over a wider range of pH values than would otherwise be possible. So while iron (in ferric sodium), manganese, and zinc are not normally available to plants in alkaline soils, they are when combined with EDTA as a chelate.	Zinc, manganese, and iron come from mines, while EDTA is a relatively safe chemical composed of carbon, hydrogen, nitrogen, and oxygen. Although iron EDTA is the most common, iron EDDHA and iron DTPA are two alternative types of iron chelates. Both deliver iron to plants more effectively than EDTA when the soil's pH is higher than 7.0.

—Jeff Gillman

Healthy root system

Water-absorbing gel

✓ **CONTAINER GARDEN**

✓ **HOW-TO**

✓ **LOW-MAINTENANCE IDEAS**

CHOOSING THE RIGHT
SOILLESS MIX

Successful container gardening means using a planting medium that ensures plant roots get a healthy balance of water and air. To help you choose the best mix, associate professor of horticulture Jim Garner identifies what to look for based on your plants' needs.

THE TERM "POTTING SOIL" HAS BECOME SOMETHING OF A misnomer in today's world of container gardening. Most bags of potting soil contain no field soil but are composed of a variety of organic and inorganic materials and are referred to as soilless mixes. As a commercial greenhouse operator and horticultural researcher, I've worked with all kinds of soilless mixes over the years and believe them to be far superior to soil-based mixes for a variety of reasons. Many excellent brands are readily available at chain stores and garden centers. If you have a clear understanding of the requirements for a good container medium and the various ingredients used in these products, choosing the right mix for your container plantings is in the bag.

Composted pine bark

Perlite

BOTH ORGANIC AND INORGANIC
INGREDIENTS SERVE A PURPOSE

Generally, most container plants will thrive in a mix that contains about 40 percent peat moss, 20 percent pine bark, 20 percent vermiculite, and 20 percent perlite or sand.

Peat moss

Composted pine bark

Coir

ORGANIC INGREDIENTS

Some organic ingredients, such as peat moss, provide needed water-holding capacity, and others, like pine bark, can lend a porous structure to avoid compaction.

Peat moss The physical and chemical properties of peat moss make it an ideal base for most soilless mixes because it can hold both water and air. It's light, but its fibrous structure allows it to hold 15 to 20 times its weight in water. The peat fibers also give it a large amount of pore space (80 to 90 percent of its total volume). It holds nutrients well, and it readily shares them with the roots, thanks to its slightly acidic pH. Horticultural-grade peats come from the decomposed remains of sphagnum moss species that have accumulated over centuries in peat bogs. They are not a renewable resource, however, and concerns about the sustainability of harvesting this product is a

common topic of discussion among gardeners. Another type of peat that is used in soilless mixes is known as reed-sedge peat, but this material is generally inferior to sphagnum peat.

Composted pine bark This material is a renewable resource and is one of the most widely used components in commercial container media, although barks from many other species are also processed for this purpose. Bark lacks the moisture-holding capacity of peat moss, but it can dramatically increase the porosity of a mix. Bark particles used in container media generally range in size from dustlike to about ⅜ inch in diameter.

Coir Another renewable organic material is coir, a derivative of coconut hulls that shows promise as a peat substitute. Coir has exceptional water-holding capacity, and when mixed with pine bark, it can eliminate or substantially reduce the need for peat moss in a mix.

Sand   Vermiculite   Perlite

Other options Other sources of organic matter that can be used in soilless mixes include composted manures, leaf mold, and crop residues such as rice hulls.

INORGANIC INGREDIENTS

Inorganic ingredients like sand, vermiculite, and perlite generally lend porosity to a mix, but they can also help retain moisture and add weight or density.

Sand This material can add needed weight to peat- and bark-based mixes and fill large pore spaces without impairing drainage. Coarse sand is preferred in most cases, and sand ground from granite is used in the best mixes. Fine sand with rounded grains like that found at the beach can actually reduce drainage when used in excessive amounts.

Vermiculite A mineral that has been heated until it expands into small accordion-shaped particles, vermiculite holds large amounts of both air and water. But it can easily be compacted, so avoid packing down mixes containing large quantities of it. Vermiculite can also retain nutrients and help a mix resist changes in pH.

Perlite One of the more common ingredients in commercial potting mixes, perlite is an inert ingredient manufactured by heating a volcanic material to produce lightweight white particles. It promotes good drainage while holding nearly as much water as vermiculite.

Other options Other inorganic materials that are useful in potting media include polystyrene (plastic) beads and calcined clay, which is similar to kitty litter. Plastic beads are inert and serve only to promote drainage, but calcined-clay particles can actually improve the moisture- and nutrient-holding capacity of a mix.

THE RIGHT BALANCE

Successful container gardening requires a potting medium that meets several of the plant's needs. The medium must be a stable reservoir of moisture and nutrients and remain loose enough to allow for root and water movement and the exchange of gases in the root zone. A growing medium must also have a pH (a measure of the alkalinity or acidity of a medium) that can support adequate nutrient uptake, and it must be free of soil-borne diseases, weed seeds, and toxins. Finally, a container medium must provide adequate anchorage and support for the roots while still being heavy enough to provide sufficient ballast to prevent plants from tipping over. A well-blended soilless medium can easily satisfy all these requirements and do so without the inherent problems and variability frequently encountered when field, or native, soils are used in containers (see the sidebar on the facing page).

If you have a good mix, water will penetrate it quickly and drain freely from the bottom of the pot. When the excess water has drained away, air will fill the large pore spaces, but enough water will be retained in the smaller spaces to provide ample moisture for the plant. In a poor mix, water may be slow to penetrate, the medium will become heavy and waterlogged, and a crust from algae or accumulated salts may form on the surface. Under these conditions, the roots become starved for oxygen, plant growth slows, foliage may begin to yellow, and plants often succumb to root rot.

FERTILIZING IS UP TO YOU

Soilless mixes have little natural fertility, so they need fertilizer, lime, and sometimes other materials added to them to give the plants nutrients. Many soilless mixes contain a "starter charge" of fertilizer that can satisfy the nutritional requirements of plants for a few weeks, but longer-term fertility maintenance can require the addition of liquid fertilizers on a regular basis. Another option is the application of a slow-release fertilizer, which provides a constant supply of available nutrients and can either be incorporated into the medium or simply top-dressed on the surface. The rate of nutrient release for most of these fertilizers is regulated by temperature, so plants receive

> ❋ ❋
>
> ## FOR THE
> ## BEST RESULTS
>
> - Lightly moisten the mix before filling containers.
> - Don't pack the mix too tightly when planting.
> - Water your pots thoroughly after planting.
> - Begin fertilizing your pots two to three weeks after planting if you did not include a slow-release fertilizer at planting time.
>
> ❋ ❋

more fertilizer when they are actively growing, and frequent watering will not leach the nutrients from the mix. Slow-release fertilizers are available in various formulations that can provide adequate nutrition for as short as three months or as long as two years.

Soilless mixes also have limited reserves of trace elements, so for best results, choose a fertilizer that also contains these micronutrients. Some mixes now come with slow-release fertilizers incorporated into the medium, and in these cases, the fertilizer analysis is usually included on the bag's label.

Most commercial mixes have ample lime added, so the pH should remain fairly stable over time. Soilless media perform well at a slightly acidic pH, so the lime requirements for these mixes are not as critical as for native garden soils. When in doubt about the fertility of a soilless mix, a soil test may be useful, but be sure to indicate that you have an artificial or greenhouse medium when submitting your samples.

Many soilless mixes have either liquid surfactants or gel-forming granules added to help them retain moisture (see the photo on the facing page). If you have trouble keeping containers well watered in hot weather or in sunny locations, you may want to consider adding one of these products to your mix before you plant. As with fertilizers, follow the label directions and don't overapply. Soilless mixes that already have extra wetting agents typically indicate this on the label.

One positive trend in soilless media products is improved labeling on the bags. Many products now list all the ingredients and additives on the package (mixes with systemic insecticides added are always clearly labeled). If you have an understanding of what components do in a mix, then choosing the right product for your container gardening needs has never been easier.

Use crystal polymers to help retain moisture.

Too much water-absorbing material, which expands greatly when moistened, can knock your plants out of their container.

WHY DON'T NATIVE SOILS BELONG IN POTS?

Field soils can be appropriate for growing plants in the garden, but these soils are unsuited for growing plants in containers. In most cases, the texture of field soils is simply too fine to ensure adequate aeration in containers, and pots or planters of any size are generally too shallow to permit proper drainage. Soilless media have larger particles, which form bigger spaces or pores to hold air in the medium while still retaining enough water for plants to survive.

SPACE-SAVING COMPOSTING SYSTEM

I come from a long line of gardeners. My grandparents, in the ways of the old country, grew most of the fruits and vegetables that reached our table. My grandfather kept a fenced-off area behind the garage known as the manure pile, which was actually two bins where manure, yard trimmings, and vegetable scraps from the kitchen found their way. Fresh stuff was placed into one bin, a month or so later it went into the other bin, and after another month it went into the garden. Because I (or one of my cousins) did most of the shoveling, I learned firsthand how much work making compost could be. I also learned that the final product—clean-smelling, rich, loose material, full of worms—could boost a plant's production, significantly increasing growth and yield.

Over the years, I've experimented with many methods of composting. My grandfather's two-bin approach worked well but had some problems. Not everything decomposed at the same rate; some material was still in its original form after two months and had to be returned to the bin. Despite my shoveling from bin to bin, the compost was not getting enough air, which led to slow decomposition.

The common way to aerate compost is to turn it over with a shovel. This turning is the dreaded task that keeps many gardeners from composting at all. Drawing from my grandfather's design, I've developed a system that eliminates the need for turning and yields more compost than I can use.

THE PLATFORM

1 Set the posts. Dig four post holes: 5 feet apart for the back and front and 3¾ feet apart for the sides. Sink the 6-foot-long 4×4 posts at an appropriate depth for your soil type. (I buried mine 3 feet deep because, on Cape Cod, we have only sand to dig in.) You may want to cement in the posts for added stability.

2 Attach the back and sides. Across the back two posts, screw in three of the 5-foot-long 2×10s, leaving about 1 inch between them to allow for airflow in the bin. On each side, screw in three of the 4-foot-long 2×10s, also leaving a 1-inch space. The front may be left open to allow for wheelbar-row access or can be partially closed in using two of the 5-foot-long 2×10s.

3 Create a divider. Place the two 3¾-foot-long 2×10s in an upright position on their longest side, approximately 20 inches in from the left side. Nail the boards in place from the rear. If you have attached the front section, nail the divider in from the front as well. For added support, drive a stake into the ground on either side of the divider.

4 Screw in the support. Attach the 3-foot-long 1×1 support using three 2-inch screws to the right side of the bin, about 5 inches below the top. This piece will support the screen on a slope.

5 Place the top. For the top of the platform, nail down the three 5¼-foot-long 2×10s starting from the rear, leaving 1 inch between them.

THE SIFTING SCREEN

1 Make the frame. Screw together the 2×4s using the 3-inch screws to make a rectangle roughly 2 feet long by 4 feet wide.

2 Affix the screen. Staple hardware cloth to the bottom side of the rectangle to create a screen.

3 Attach a runner to the frame. Screw in the 2-foot-long 1×1 using two 2-inch screws across the bottom of the screen, about 10 inches from one end, to make the runner. This piece rides along the divider and allows the screen to move back and forth.

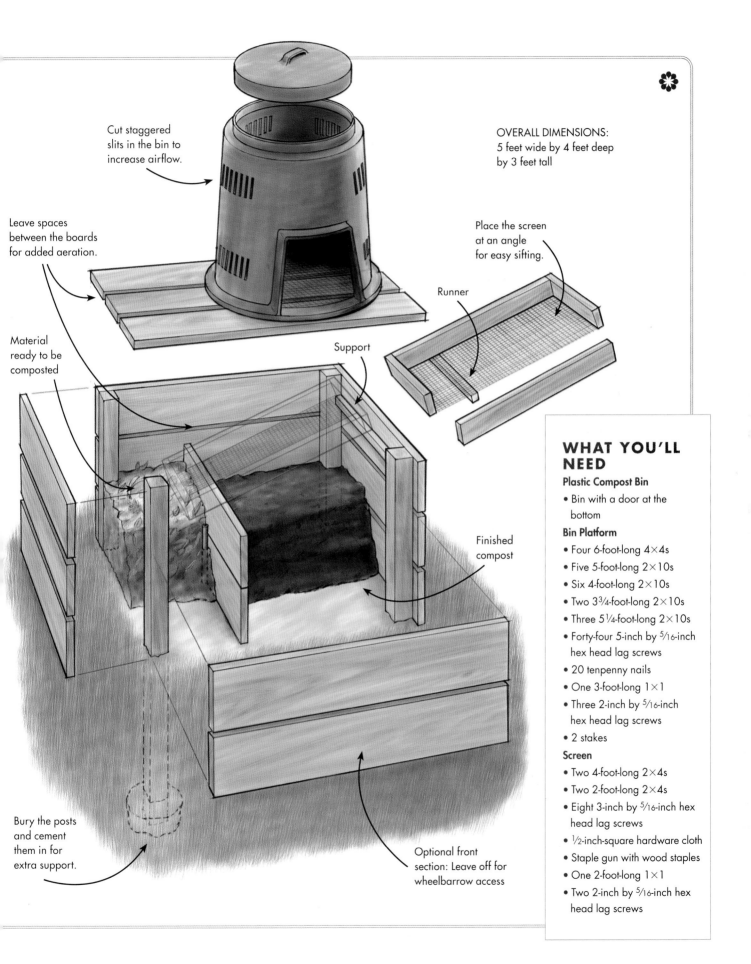

Cut staggered slits in the bin to increase airflow.

OVERALL DIMENSIONS:
5 feet wide by 4 feet deep by 3 feet tall

Leave spaces between the boards for added aeration.

Place the screen at an angle for easy sifting.

Runner

Material ready to be composted

Support

Finished compost

Bury the posts and cement them in for extra support.

Optional front section: Leave off for wheelbarrow access

WHAT YOU'LL NEED

Plastic Compost Bin
- Bin with a door at the bottom

Bin Platform
- Four 6-foot-long 4×4s
- Five 5-foot-long 2×10s
- Six 4-foot-long 2×10s
- Two 3¾-foot-long 2×10s
- Three 5¼-foot-long 2×10s
- Forty-four 5-inch by ⁵⁄₁₆-inch hex head lag screws
- 20 tenpenny nails
- One 3-foot-long 1×1
- Three 2-inch by ⁵⁄₁₆-inch hex head lag screws
- 2 stakes

Screen
- Two 4-foot-long 2×4s
- Two 2-foot-long 2×4s
- Eight 3-inch by ⁵⁄₁₆-inch hex head lag screws
- ½-inch-square hardware cloth
- Staple gun with wood staples
- One 2-foot-long 1×1
- Two 2-inch by ⁵⁄₁₆-inch hex head lag screws

Give your plants a drink and make life easier by using drip irrigation in your containers.

✓ HOW-TO
✓ ECO-FRIENDLY OPTION
✓ LOW-MAINTENANCE IDEAS

WATER WISELY
WITH DRIP IRRIGATION

Assembling a watering system yourself saves time and money, and once installer T.A. Johnson guides you through the design and installation process, you can design a system for any size garden— or even a collection of containers.

WHEN MY WIFE AND I PLANTED ORNAMENTAL GARDENS IN Sandy, Utah, we knew we'd have to irrigate our plants somehow. For several years, we watered with a hose and sprinkler, but that got old in a hurry. We considered in-ground sprinkler systems, but they seemed costly and wasteful of water. Then I learned about the merits of drip irrigation. With a series of carefully placed emitters, water could be delivered right to the root zones of plants. And we could enjoy the convenience of a permanent watering system.

Water is a finite natural resource. As populations increase in North America, many areas are facing water shortages and periodic droughts. These crises make a water-thrifty garden irrigation system an attractive tool. With a drip system, my plants thrive with less water. Keeping water off foliage also cuts down on fungal diseases. When I occasionally use pesticides, they aren't washed off when the system kicks in. And, since only the roots of plants of my choosing get watered, many fewer weeds pop up. With a simple drip-irrigation system, you can water perennials, annuals, shrubs, trees, ground covers, and even potted plants.

FLEXIBLE PARTS MAKE CONSTRUCTION SIMPLE

Think of a drip-irrigation system as an upscale soaker hose. But instead of water spraying out every 2 inches, it can seep out every foot—or maybe every 3 feet—drip by drip. With a little planning, those drips can line up with the root zones of plants.

Drip-irrigation parts snap together like modular toys and can be adjusted as your garden changes (see the photos at right). You'll need a filter, water-pressure reducer, hose swivels, emitters, and $1/2$- or $5/8$-inch flexible polyethylene tubing—also called the submain. You may need a backflow preventer if it's required by your municipal water department. Optional parts include $1/4$-inch solid tubing, $1/4$-inch drip line, connecting tees, 90-degree elbows, connecting barbs, hold-downs to keep tubing in place, goof plugs to fill holes you decide not to use, timers, and fertilizer injectors. You can buy these parts at some hardware stores or garden centers, or from companies specializing in irrigation systems. Parts from different manufacturers are almost always interchangeable.

System costs are very reasonable. For installation, all you need are strong shears to cut the tubing, and a 16-penny nail or commercial punch to poke holes in the submain for the emitters and $1/4$-inch tubing. You can bury the submain just below the soil or leave it on the surface and cover it with mulch. Either way, I try to run it along the edge of a bed so I won't accidentally disturb it. The $1/4$-inch tubing can also be buried, but leave drip lines on the surface so the emitters don't clog with soil. I use a combination of buried and mulched lines in my garden, so only small emitters are visible here and there.

You can convert an existing sprinkler system to drip irrigation by plugging all the spray heads on a circuit but one and running a drip circuit from that one head. Remember to choose circuits that aren't needed to water the lawn. There are two critical points to keep in mind. First, drip irrigation works on low pressure—from 10 to 30 pounds per square inch (psi). However, water pressure at hose spigots runs anywhere from 50 to 100 psi, so you need a pressure reducer on every drip-irrigation circuit. Second, as a conservative rule, any one drip-irrigation circuit can only handle about 225 gallons per hour, so you'll need to calculate the total gph for all emitters on each drip circuit to make sure they don't exceed this amount. Each emitter has its own rating, so simply add up the numbers.

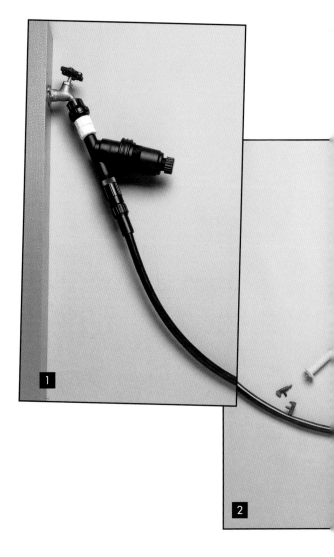

ASSESS YOUR WATERING NEEDS BEFORE YOU START TO BUILD

Use a tape measure to roughly determine how much flexible tubing you'll need for the submain. Start at the hose spigot and work your way through your garden. The total run of submain on any one drip-irrigation circuit should not exceed 400 feet. While the tubing is flexible, for a 90-degree turn you'll need an elbow. If you want to branch the submain, use a connecting tee.

Wherever the submain runs within a few inches of a plant, you can snap in an emitter to provide water. The emitter has a connecting barb on one end. To water a plant further from the submain, put a barb in the submain, attach $1/4$-inch solid tubing to the barb, then put an emitter on the other end.

Figuring how many emitters you'll need is not a hard-and-fast proposition. You'll have to consider your soil

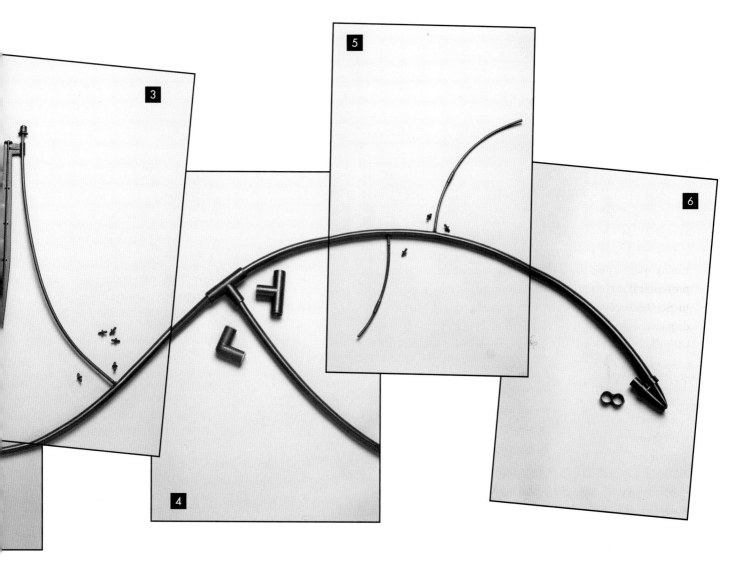

1 Attach a drip-irrigation system to a hose bib. The heart of the system is an assembly that includes an adapter, filter, pressure reducer, and coupler. The submain—flexible, hoselike tubing—forms the system's main water-carrying artery. Warm the tubing in the sun to make it more pliable and easier to install.

2 Deliver water to plants with an emitter. Attach one to the submain by using a commercial punch (above), or a 16-penny nail to make holes in the submain. Then push the barbed point of an emitter through the hole. Emitters come in various styles and sizes, with output ranging from 1 to 4 gallons per hour.

3 Sprinkler-type emitters can be used to water a larger area. They can be fitted on ¼-inch tubing attached to the submain with connecting barbs. Stakes can hold the tubing and emitter above ground.

4 Branch the system with connecting tees. Use elbows to turn tight corners. Because you can add components anywhere along the submain, drip-irrigation systems permit you to alter the design during initial installation, or later, as the garden changes.

5 Use drip lines to water beds. Drip lines use built-in emitters that each usually put out ½ gph; the pre-punched holes are spaced a foot apart in ¼-inch tubing.

6 Seal off open ends on all water lines. Here, a figure-eight-style seal secures the end of a submain. Ends of ¼-inch tubing can be bent and tied off with a piece of wire.

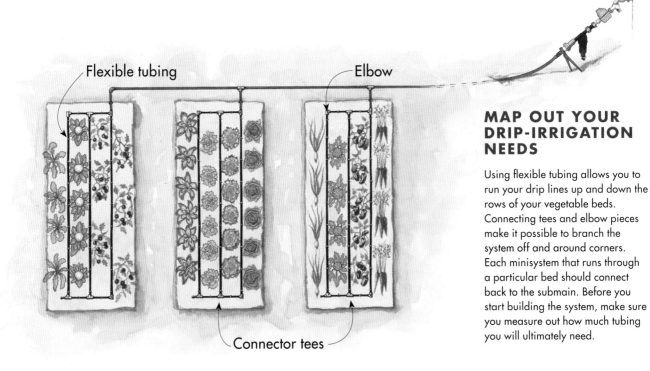

Flexible tubing

Elbow

Connector tees

MAP OUT YOUR DRIP-IRRIGATION NEEDS

Using flexible tubing allows you to run your drip lines up and down the rows of your vegetable beds. Connecting tees and elbow pieces make it possible to branch the system off and around corners. Each minisystem that runs through a particular bed should connect back to the submain. Before you start building the system, make sure you measure out how much tubing you will ultimately need.

type, the plants' sizes and general water needs, your garden's microclimates, and whether you use mulch. A 1-gph emitter will cover an area 12 inches in diameter in sandy soil or an area 18 inches in diameter in clay soil. I generally give 1-gallon-size plants a single 1-gph emitter right on the root ball. With larger plants, I start with one 1-gph emitter per foot of branch-spread diameter. Got a 4-foot-diameter bush? Space four 1-gph emitters halfway between the trunk and the drip line. I use 1-gph emitters because it's easier to keep track of how many gph are on any given line.

For entire beds, I use 1/4-inch drip-line tubing with built-in 1/2-gph emitters every 12 inches (see the photo on the facing page). This tubing attaches to the submain with a connecting barb; each line can snake up to 50 feet through a bed. Drip lines work best with a 25-psi pressure reducer.

To get the equivalent of an inch of rainwater from a 1-gph emitter takes just shy of an hour. In our hot Utah climate, 2 inches of water per week is recommended during the growing season. Consult a county extension agent for the recommendation in your area.

OVERWINTER YOUR SYSTEM

Maintenance for a drip system is fairly simple. If you live where it freezes in winter, disconnect the line from the spigot in the fall and take the backflow preventer, pressure reducer, and filter inside. The other tubing is flexible and should not split when frozen. Tie plastic wrap over the end of the submain.

In spring, open the end of the submain, and flush the system to get rid of debris. In a warm climate, your entire system may remain in place year-round. I've used drip irrigation for six years now and everything from petunias to pine trees is doing just fine, thank you. And, as a bonus, my water bills are lower than most of my neighbors'.

Give your beds a drink and your wallet a break. If you're installing a drip system for an entire bed, place emitters every 12 inches to be sure that your soil stays evenly moist.

Individual plants are the best indicators of how long you need to water. If plants look the worse for wear at 5 p.m. on a hot, sunny day, that's pretty common. But if the same plants still look wilted early the next morning, you need to investigate. You can check soil moisture with an old screwdriver. In damp soil, it's easy to push in the screwdriver. In dry soil, you'll need help from a big hammer. If the soil is dry, then your plants aren't getting enough water. Run the system longer each time, or add more emitters. If the soil is wet, then you might be overwatering. Pay special attention to new plants because their roots haven't spread out in the soil yet. Just because the soil is damp a few inches from a new plant doesn't mean the plant is getting any water.

It's best to water deeply but infrequently. If there are puddles by emitters, you've run your system too long. Instead, you should see a small area of damp earth. Below the surface, where roots can go as deep as 18 inches, water will spread out and sink into the soil.

All this from seed? Sowing right in the ground is easy and doesn't require any special equipment—except something to carry all the vegetables you'll be harvesting.

DIRECT SOWING
MADE EASY

Get the most from your space by sowing some seeds in the ground. Horticulturist Jennifer Benner teaches you how to do it so you get the most from your space—allowing you to save time and money.

EVEN THOUGH I CONSIDER MYSELF A THRIFTY SHOPPER, I OFTEN leave the grocery store feeling a lot lighter in the wallet. I just won't compromise on some things, like healthy, organic produce. To cut costs, I began growing my own vegetables several years ago by filling my plot with young plants from a local farm stand, eventually graduating to growing my own inexpensive and easy vegetables from seed.

Growing veggies from seed allows you to have more culinary diversity and to spread out your planting time to enjoy successional harvests. All veggies can be grown from seed, but those that are sown directly in the garden tend to be the easiest. You can try your hand at growing row and mound veggies and get great results, all without putting in the extra effort that indoor seed starting often entails.

MOST SEEDS NEED
A SHALLOW TRENCH

Directly sowing vegetable seeds usually involves spacing
them evenly in a shallow trench once the soil temperature
reaches roughly 50°F to 60°F (see the photo below). The
depth of the trench and exact soil temperature depend on
the vegetable, so be sure to follow planting recommenda-
tions. Start with good soil and a weed-free bed, turning a
2- to 3-inch-deep layer of compost into the entire planting area. Most vegetable gardeners recommend doing
this step in the fall to give the compost a chance to break
down, but I often run out of time and believe that fortify-
ing soil in the spring is better than not doing it at all. No
matter when I put the compost down, I always fertilize in
the spring, applying a naturally derived granular fertilizer.

   Using the corner of a hoe or similar hand tool, I cut
a shallow furrow and place seeds at the suggested spacing, gently covering them with soil. For tiny seeds, I use
a handheld seed sower. To keep track of my rows, I place

Start with a shallow
trench and a
handful of seeds.

EASY VEGGIES FROM SEED

NAME	RECOMMENDED VARIETIES	CARE TIPS	HARVEST
SOW BELOWGROUND			
BUSH BEANS	'Provider' and 'Bush Blue Lake'	Bush beans require average moisture and moderately rich soil. Inoculated seeds are reported to yield up to twice as many beans. For a continuous harvest, sow seed every two weeks until 8 to 10 weeks from fall frost.	50 to 70 days after germination, depending on the variety
CARROTS	'Scarlet Nantes' and 'Sugarsnax'	Carrots prefer sandy loam that can be easily penetrated by their roots. Avoid rocky and overly rich soil. Keep the soil evenly moist. For consecutive harvests, sow seed every three weeks through early summer.	55 to 95 days after germination, depending on the variety
RADISHES	'Cherry Belle' and 'Easter Egg'	Most radishes like it moist and cool. Some varieties, like 'Cherry Belle', can tolerate the summer heat and be planted every two weeks for a harvest that lasts all season long.	20 to 65 days after germination, depending on the variety
SOW IN MOUNDS			
SQUASH	'Raven' zucchini and 'Waltham' butternut squash	Give squash plenty of space, and water plants at the base to minimize the occurrence of powdery mildew. Squash are constant feeders and appreciate regular feeding and adequate moisture.	50 to 110 days after germination, depending on the variety
CUCUMBERS	'Marketmore 76' for slicing and 'National' for pickling	Cucumbers appreciate deep, regular watering. They're also heavy feeders and don't mind another taste of fertilizer midway through the season. For a plentiful harvest, they can be planted every three weeks until 12 to 14 weeks from fall frost.	50 to 80 days after germination, depending on the variety
WATERMELONS	'Sugar Baby' and 'Crimson Sweet'	Watermelons love the heat, lots of feedings, and well-drained, loamy soil. For best results, keep the soil moist and maturing fruit off the ground.	60 to 100 days after germination, depending on the variety

Thinning plants provides more room to grow. Even though you sowed them all, many seedlings should be pulled out to give the rest a better chance to grow.

a tag at one end and a stick at the other end. You can use stakes and string to guide you, but for the sake of time, I just eyeball my rows.

After planting, water your rows with a gentle spray. Keep the soil moist (but not wet) until the seed germinates. Then water regularly throughout the season using a soaker hose or drip irrigation (put in place during planting time). Overhead sprinklers are acceptable but can encourage leaf diseases.

Once your seedlings sprout, you may see that your seed spacing wasn't as good as you thought. When plants reach about 2 inches tall, thin some out by cutting them at the base with scissors to give the remaining seedlings adequate elbow room. Don't yank them: This can damage the roots of the keepers. As the seedlings gain size and the temperature rises, feel free to put down a 2- to 3-inch-deep layer of straw mulch between your rows, stopping a few inches away from the base of your plants. This will help retain moisture and inhibit weeds, keeping your veggies growing healthy and strong.

GIVE VINING VEGGIES A MOUND

Vining veggies with large seeds, such as squash, watermelon, and cucumbers, are typically planted in hills. These small mounds of soil act like mini raised beds: providing good drainage, preventing wet feet and rot during times of heavy rain, and supplying extra warmth for cold-sensitive seeds and seedlings.

I begin hill planting by thoroughly turning in a generous shovelful of compost or composted manure to a depth of 12 to 18 inches where the mound will be located. Space hills 2 to 6 feet apart, depending on what you are planting. These plants want plenty of room for good air circulation to prevent leaf diseases.

Next, I build my hills, roughly 12 to 14 inches wide and 5 to 7 inches high (see the photo on the facing page). I then gently firm the soil. Be sure to do this on a day when the soil is not overly wet or overly dry. The soil should be moist yet crumbly when squeezed in your hand, not a solid ball or collection of loose grains. The soil temperature should be 60°F to 70°F, depending on the veggie variety.

Sow six to eight seeds per hill. Follow up with a gentle soaking of water. Keep the seeds evenly moist until germination. Then water regularly throughout the season, trying to avoid getting the leaves wet.

Once the seedlings are 3 to 4 inches tall, thin out the weakest plants with a few snips of the scissors, leaving two or three plants per hill. At this point, I usually side-dress these heavy feeders with my favorite fertilizer. It's not a bad idea to mulch the bed with a 2- to 3-inch-thick layer of straw as well. Besides retaining moisture and inhibiting weeds, the mulch will help prevent fruit rot by keeping low-lying veggies from developing on the soil. To save space, vining veggies with fairly light fruit, such as cucumbers, can be trained to grow on a structure.

Growing your own veggies isn't only about food safety and the almighty dollar. It's also about freedom of choice in varieties and timing—something you don't often get when growing plants from a garden center. With your own veggie-garden supply, you'll be able to dine on fresh produce all season long.

Hill planting is hassle-free. It keeps sensitive seeds warm and soil well-drained. Mounded seeds may leave less room for creativity in planting, but large, productive vines will soon fill in the space with robust crops.

MAXIMIZE YOUR
HARVEST

Get more from your space with succession planting. All it takes is growing your own seedlings and keeping a close eye on the calendar. Gardener Pamela Bird tells you what you need to know to extend the season.

IF YOU ARE THE TYPICAL GARDENER, YOU PLANT YOUR vegetable garden in late spring and harvest from it in summer, then you clean it up in fall. But you can get two, three, possibly four crops a year from your garden, without having to use things like cold frames and greenhouses. I practice an approach known as "succession planting" to get the most from my garden space. I interplant small crops among large ones and quick-growing crops with slower ones, and I replace harvested plants with fresh, vigorous seedlings. Succession planting requires that you work in close association with your calendar and that you use transplants whenever you can.

Big changes occur from late spring (top) to summer (bottom). The pea trellis in the top right corner has given way to a teepee of beans below. Spring carrots at the rear of the second bed have made room for squash by late summer. The young tomato plants have grown quite a bit over the course of several weeks and shaded out most of the early crops at their feet.

THE SUCCESSION-PLANTING GUIDE

Get the most out of your garden by thinking of the growing season in four separate parts. In early spring, sow short-season veggies. As you harvest those in late spring, replant the holes with longer-season crops for the ultimate summer harvest. And as the warm-weather plants fade, replant the empty spaces with short-season crops once again.

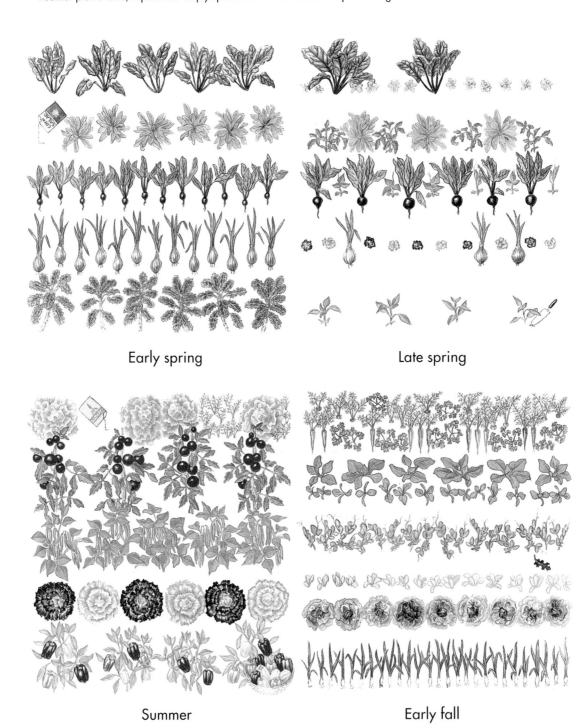

Early spring

Late spring

Summer

Early fall

TWO PLANTING TECHNIQUES ARE KEY

Interplanting and replacing not only are valuable techniques on their own but also can boost the output from your garden when they're practiced together.

Interplanting just means to mix different crops in the same bed. I interplant fast-growing crops amid slower ones and small crops among larger ones. For example, I'll surround cabbage and broccoli, which grow slowly to a large size, with onions and spring greens, which are smaller and grow quickly. As the onions and greens mature and are harvested, there's more room left for the bigger veggies. Or I'll grow lettuce close to tomatoes. By the time the tomatoes are getting large, I will have already cut the lettuce. When planning to interplant, it's important to think about the growing habits of the different crops.

Replacing harvested plants with transplants is succession gardening in its purest form. I sometimes fill a hole with the same type of plant. Lettuce is a typical example. I always keep a supply of lettuce seedlings on hand to fill in spaces left when I cut out mature heads. Other times, though, I fill the hole with something else. I'll replace winter chard or beets with tomatoes and spring greens or put summer squash where I've just harvested a cabbage. To get the best yield in my garden, I sometimes remove a

Start the next crop while the last crop matures. These cool-season peas will replace hot-season tomatoes.

TRANSPLANTS MAKE IT ALL POSSIBLE

Having healthy transplants on hand at the proper time is critical for succession planting, and that means starting them yourself. The first year, I relied on plants from nurseries, only to discover that I couldn't find the seedlings I wanted when I needed them. I began growing my own in self-defense.

Some seedlings hold better than others in trays or pots. Lettuce plants especially need to be transplanted soon or else they'll get leggy, so I try to get them into the garden within a month of sowing. Tomatoes, peas, and beans get transplanted from the seed trays at four to six weeks. Cabbage and broccoli hold well in the seed trays as long as they get frequent watering and regular feedings.

Lettuce is a great crop to grow in succession. Plant seedlings each week for fresh salads all season long.

crop before it's finished. For example, chard can produce well in any mild climate for up to two years, but I usually yank it sooner to make room for other crops.

KNOW YOUR SEASONS, AND START SMALL

To practice succession gardening, timing is critical, particularly for the fall garden. As soon as I get in my summer crops, I begin thinking about starting seedlings for fall crops.

Pay attention to how long it takes the varieties you're growing to mature. This will help you plan ahead. For fall growing, choose varieties that mature quickly. Count back from your fall frost date the number of days or weeks to maturity—that's the date you need to have the plant settled in the garden. Now count back another six weeks. That's the date you should sow the seeds in flats.

If you're new to succession planting, start with one bed of manageable size, say 3 to 5 feet wide and 10 to 14 feet long. This will give you room to experiment with a variety of plants. Once you're familiar with the technique, you can expand into additional beds. It also helps to start with easy crops, like lettuce, tomatoes, peas, and beans. These are all fast-growing and rewarding. Leave the more difficult crops, like cabbage, until you have gained some experience. In time, you will develop a rhythm of sowing, transplanting, and harvesting that will become second nature to you.

The season doesn't end when the temperature drops. A second planting of carrots, some radishes, and even a few lettuce plants keeps the garden green and your harvest basket full as fall sets in.

Leaf

Fruit

Root

Legume

CROP ROTATION
FOR ANY GARDEN

Crop rotation might seem out of reach if you have a small space, but it's not. All you need to do is divide your space into four areas— you decide how big—and follow gardener Cynthia Hizer's advice for success.

WHERE DID I PUT THE ARUGULA TWO YEARS AGO? AND LAST year, it seems that the tomatoes were in the main garden. Or were they by the rabbit hutch? I guess I can't plant potatoes there this year—I think. If, like me, you're not keeping track of these details, you may not be getting the most out of your garden or giving your vegetables all they need. And you may be making needless work for yourself.

Moving plants around from year to year is one of the best organic techniques to minimize disease and bug problems and to maximize soil fertility. Various rotation plans are popular. The simplest is "don't plant the same thing in the same place two years in a row." This strategy is designed to ward off pests. If the cabbage-looper pupa nestles down in the cabbage debris in October and reawakens the following spring to more cabbage, that's instant sustenance. But if you've moved the cabbage, the looper may die trying to find its food.

Some gardeners move plants around by family: nightshade, brassica, and cucurbit, for example. For this system, it's helpful

COVER CROPS ARE PART OF THE PROGRAM

Cover crops are plants grown to enhance production, reduce weeds, and stimulate soil activity. When turned under, they compost right in the soil, which is why they're also called "green manure." I use cover crops during the off-season when I'm not growing vegetables and also to fill blank spaces in the beds during the growing season. I try to match the cover crop to my rotation plan.

Sow legumes—clover, vetch, or alfalfa—in the legume bed after the harvest to boost the nitrogen for the incoming leaf crop.

After the leaf crops are harvested, sow wheat, which discourages diseases and nematodes that might plague next year's tomatoes and peppers. Mow the wheat when it's about 8 inches tall, leave it on the bed over the winter, and turn it under in the spring.

After the fruiting crops are finished, scatter rye seeds over the empty bed. The decaying rye roots leave the ground fluffy, perfect for growing shapely carrots and beets from the roots group that will grow in that bed the following year.

In the hiatus between spring and fall root crops, plant buckwheat, a grain that thrives in summer heat. Buckwheat discourages weeds and also loosens the soil. I'm careful to mow buckwheat before it flowers; otherwise, it will become a weed. After the fall roots are harvested, I'm back to planting legumes.

to have a working knowledge of Latin as well as an intimate knowledge of plant parts. One well-known gardening expert suggests a 10-year rotation. But I get dizzy just thinking of the complications. What if I sell the house before 10 years are up? Should the rotation plan be in my will?

I use a system that's easy to implement and easy to remember without a notebook. I separate my crops based on their nutritional requirements. It so happens that the plants fall pretty neatly into leafy crops, fruiting crops, and root crops. A fourth division is for legumes—peas and beans—which technically are fruits, but they get their own plot because they actually add more nutrients to the soil than they take. By default, this system separates families and thus helps diminish pest problems. Leaf, fruit, root, legume—that's my crop-rotation plan. No detailed plant anatomy, no bookkeeping, and no Latin (which I still plan to learn someday).

TEST THE SOIL, THEN AMEND

I started by having my soil tested at a lab. I then added the recommended amounts of nutrients—manure, compost, black rock phosphate, greensand, gypsum, and lime—to my entire garden. I did this in fall so that the amendments would have time to break down and become available to the plants.

In spring, I divided the garden into four sections and planted each with one of the following groups: leaf, fruit, root, or legume. Every year, I now rotate the plantings so that the leaf group moves to where the legumes grew the season before, and the other groups all move over a section.

Having four areas of roughly equal size makes this system work, even though you'll probably want to grow more of one kind of crop than another. I made each division big enough to hold the largest group that I grow, and I fill the empty spaces in my less-crowded sections with cover crops. If the areas aren't the same size, you'll be tempted, when it comes time to put the largest group—say, the fruits—into a too-small space, to sneak some extra tomatoes or peppers into an area where they don't belong. And then your nice, neat system will have been breached.

Another benefit to this rotation system is that it's easy to remember when and where to add soil amendments. Every fall, I amend only the bed that will hold next year's leaf crop. First, I get my soil tested, then I add manure and

Leaf crops use nitrogen.

Fruit crops use phosphorus.

Root crops use potassium.

Legumes add nitrogen.

whatever amendments the test results recommend—lime, rock phosphate, greensand. At this time, I also spread compost over the entire garden. This program is based on using organic amendments, which stay in the soil longer than nonorganic fertilizers. If you're not using cover crops, you'll need to add manure to each bed every year.

LEAF CROPS

Leaves love nitrogen, so the plants in this group need plenty of nitrogen to build strong stems and leaves. Nitrogen is the most readily soluble of all the nutrients and, therefore, the hardest for the soil to hold on to. So it's important to grow leaf crops in soil that's had a fresh infusion of nitrogen. Manure or a cover crop (see the

sidebar on the facing page) is the cornerstone. During the growing season, I also give the plants in the leaf bed some extra amendments (fish or blood meal).

FRUIT CROPS

For fruit, phosphorus is a must. Everything that develops as a result of a flower being pollinated is a fruit. These crops need a generous amount of phosphorus to set blossoms and to develop fruit. If the soil is rich in nitrogen, the leaves will be luxurious, but flowers and fruit will be few. Bonemeal and rock phosphate are the best sources of phosphorus to add to your soil, if a test indicates a low amount. Bonemeal breaks down sooner than rock phosphate and needs to be renewed more often. Rock

FOLLOW THE FOUR-BED PLANT PLAN

Each year move the crop that was in bed 1 to bed 4. That will open bed 1 up, and you can shift each bed's crop down. In other words, bed 2 crops move to bed 1, bed 3 crops move to bed 2, and bed 4 crops move to bed 3.

	BED 1	BED 2	BED 3	BED 4
CROP TYPE	Leaf	Fruit	Root	Legume
CROP EXAMPLES	Mesclun greens, herbs, cabbage, kale, broccoli, cauliflower, spinach	Tomatoes, cucumbers, squash, peppers, eggplants	Radishes, carrots, turnips, beets, onions, leeks	Peas, beans
HONORARY MEMBER	Corn	Garlic		Potatoes
WINTER COVER CROP	Wheat	Rye	Buckwheat	Clover, vetch, or alfalfa

phosphate is my favorite; it takes a year to become fully available, but one application lasts five years.

ROOT CROPS

Roots rely mainly on potassium. At the same time, they need even less nitrogen than fruit. That's fine because, by the third year of my rotation plan, most of the nitrogen has been used up in a given bed, but the leisurely potassium is ready and waiting to go to work. If I need to add potassium, my favorite source are greens, because it also yields dozens of trace minerals and helps break up clay soil. Wood ashes, gypsum, kelp, and granite dust are also good sources of potassium.

LEGUME CROPS

Legumes put nitrogen back into the soil. Beans and peas pull nitrogen from the air and store it on their roots. I grow these in the last bed of the cycle because when their roots decompose in the soil, the nitrogen becomes available for the following year's leaf crop. The spent plants, when turned into the garden, add organic matter.

EVERY RULE HAS ITS EXCEPTIONS

I've had a hard time deciding where to put corn, potatoes, and garlic, but I'm happy with what I'm doing now. Corn is a heavy user of nitrogen, so I grow it in the leaf rotation, even though corn is a fruiting crop. In fact, I plant corn seed right into my lettuce patch; the growing corn shades the lettuce and takes over when the lettuce is finished.

Potatoes are roots, but they are also in the nightshade family, which includes tomatoes, peppers, and eggplants. I noticed that the potatoes suffered more pest problems when they followed their relatives. I now plant potatoes in the legume bed, which keeps them two years away from their kin.

And, finally, garlic is a little awkward because its growing season stretches from fall to summer. I now plant garlic in October in the fruit bed, which will be the root bed the following year.

PRUNING SECRETS TO KEEP A TREE SMALL

A tree's leader is its central, dominant stem, and the first step is to cut it back and find a replacement. Nature will see to it that my choice for the new leader straightens out and becomes dominant. The highest branch tip on a limb sends chemicals down through the wood, ensuring that this tip has the edge on the others and dominates the limb's resources. It will begin to grow more quickly than those around it and, in the case of a new leader, will become more vertical. The same holds true for the side branches: The tallest shoot on the branch will have an advantage, so shortening the others gives the edge to the one I prefer.

If I don't choose a new leader, nature will, and this choice will be growing in a more horizontal direction. The result is a tree that is off-center. Another reason to choose a new leader is that there could be several candidates for the position, all at the same height and none with a clear dominance over the others. You then wind up with a bushy top that looks like a bird's nest.

I don't cut just to my desired outline; instead I make the cut far enough back on the branch that growth beginning from the new tip can continue for at least one season without exceeding the height or spread limit I've set for the tree. Pruning the interior branches maintains the treelike appearance, so after heading back each main branch, I work back along the branch to shorten the side branches.

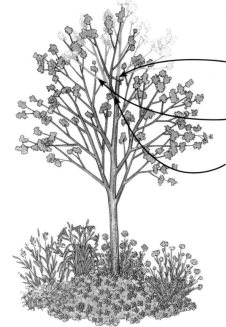

CUT THE LEADER TO LIMIT HEIGHT

1 Cut off the leader—the dominant stem—at the beginning of its new growth.

2 Choose a healthy branch near the top to be the new leader.

3 Carefully bend the new leader up and tie it to the stump of the old leader. Wide cloth ties, hook-and-loop fasteners, or even old nylon stockings serve nicely as tying materials.

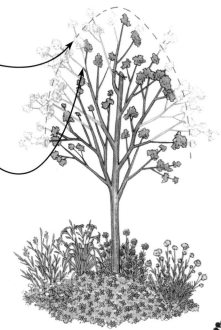

SHAPE THE SIDES

1 Stand back and draw an imaginary outline of the tree you want from the new tip to the ground. Branches that cross that outline need to be pruned.

2 To cut back a branch on a tree, prune to just above a side branch that is well-placed to become the new tip.

2

EDIBLE GARDENS

Edibles create a striking harvest. The tall, vibrant red shoots of 'Hopi Red Dye' amaranth and 'Rubra' orach along with the purple stalk and lacy leaves of 'Redbor' kale are deliciously ornamental.

✓ ADD COLOR
✓ DESIGN IDEAS
✓ PLANT SUGGESTIONS

MIXING EDIBLES
WITH ORNAMENTALS

Vegetables don't have to be relegated to a separate garden. In fact, gardening author Nancy J. Ondra argues you should choose your edibles at the same time you choose your ornamentals. After all, with their great texture and shapes, edibles can enhance your design as well as any ornamental can.

IN THE QUEST TO FIND SOMETHING NEW AND DIFFERENT FOR your garden each spring, it's easy to zoom right past the offerings of veggie seeds and transplants on your way to the glitzier displays of flower-filled annuals and perennials. Don't be too quick, though, to dismiss vegetables as merely practical plants. If you consider them purely from a design standpoint—for their interesting form, their colorful leaves, their dramatic blooms, and their showy fruit—you'll see that many vegetables easily rival more traditional ornamentals. And they have the advantage of being tasty as well as attractive.

There's nothing new, of course, about blurring the line between edible and ornamental plantings. That's a cornerstone of the traditional cottage-garden style and of a potager. It's a little different, though, to look first at vegetables for their decorative features, then make allowances for the possibility of picking them. The primary point here isn't raising enough food to feed your family through the winter or making dramatic design statements with artfully patterned vegetable plantings. It's the joy of creating exciting combinations and beautiful gardens with plants that you could pick if you have the time and desire to do so.

So what sets the best edibles apart from the rest? They're undeniably ornamental even if you never harvest from them. They may have distinctive foliage that contributes color or texture over an extended period or even through the entire growing season. They may have striking flower forms that are guaranteed to grab interest from bud stage through seed formation. Or they may produce an abundance of long-lasting fruit that take on rich colors as they ripen. And the best edibles—the pick of the crop, as it were—combine two or more of these traits in one plant.

ADD VEGGIES FOR A BOLD STATEMENT

A number of plants from the family Brassicaceae (also known as Cruciferae) have long been prized for their edible parts—specifically, in the case of cabbage, kale, and

Surprise garden visitors with cabbage as your border edging. The spreading leaves mimic a hosta's outward growth, but the mounded heads provide more interest.

Brussels sprouts, for their nutritious foliage. But even if you don't relish the thought of eating them, these brassicas offer some absolutely stunning shapes and leaf textures, contributing height, mass, and color to ornamental combinations.

In sunny gardens, for instance, plants such as cabbage and its nonheading relatives Portuguese kale (*Brassica oleracea* var. *tronchuda*, annual) and 'Red Russian' kale (*Brassica napus* var. *pabularia* 'Red Russian', annual) fill the role that hostas (*Hosta* spp. and cvs., USDA Hardiness Zones 3–9) perform so admirably in shade gardens: providing broad mounds of large leaves to counterbalance an abundance of tiny or lacy leaves and flowers. And the bold, rounded heads of maturing cabbage stop traffic in their own right, creating a dramatic accent that's unlike anything you can get from a traditional ornamental.

Kale is another brassica that doesn't get much respect as a vegetable—let alone as an ornamental—but it's invaluable for its height and form. The ultimate height varies by variety, but when you plant out seedlings in spring and let them grow through the whole season, some can easily reach 3 to 4 feet tall by fall. That allows you to plant them in the middle of the border, where their broad foliage clumps can rise through the seasons as their companions mature. Placing lower, bushy plants in front of the kale gives you the option of harvesting the lower kale leaves through the summer without leaving visible bare stems. Good choices for tall-growing kales are 'Redbor' and 'Winterbor'.

Kales offer a range of leaf textures as well. Many are strongly crinkled or frilly on the edges; others, such as Russian types (which mature at about 18 inches tall), have flatter, jagged-edged foliage. 'Nero di Toscana' is great for foliage as well as height, with long, slender leaves that have a distinctive pebbly texture.

Brussels sprouts may elicit groans at the dinner table, but they're more likely to inspire wows in the border. Starting out as loose, low heads of broad leaves, like cabbage, they also grow upward, like some types of kale, usually to about 30 inches by the end of the growing season. By late summer, the sprouts, which resemble miniature cabbages, form at the leaf joints along the stout main stem, adding even more interest. You can surround the plants with low companions to get the full effect of a leafy topknot above the knobby stem, or you could use bushier companions and just enjoy the leafy tops as mid-border accents.

Which plants aren't the ornamental? 'Redbor' kale and 'Bright Lights' chard look right at home with black-eyed Susans.

GOOD BEDFELLOWS

Reita Jackson has found that some plants pair well, either for aesthetic reasons or because one provides a cultural benefit to the other. The latter, known as "companion planting," is described in *Roses Love Garlic* by Louise Riotte. Reita's gardening lore has also been passed down to her by her mother and mother-in-law. —Reita Jackson

MARIGOLDS AND TOMATOES

Strongly scented marigolds repel insects and help tomatoes grow more productively. Grown beneath tomatoes, marigolds also suppress weeds.

MORNING GLORIES AND CORN

Morning glories attract hoverflies, which feed on aphids, thus keeping the pests away from corn.

NASTURTIUMS AND CABBAGE

Nasturtiums repel squash bugs and other insects that attack cabbage, cucumbers, and squash.

CHIVES AND ROSES

Members of the *Allium* genus, such as chives, garlic, and onions, protect their companions from insects and deter rabbits from a garden.

SUNFLOWERS AND CORN

Sunflowers attract aphids away from corn and are said to increase its yield. In addition, the two tall plants look attractive growing together.

It's an eye grabber. Brussels sprouts makes an ornamental impact as well as any bold-leaved tropical.

Cabbage-family crops grow quickly, so you get the full effect of their ornamental qualities in just one growing season. While they are technically biennials (producing flowers and seeds the following year), it's best to treat them as annuals, harvesting the usable parts when you do fall cleanup or removing the plants in fall or early spring, then replanting.

If you'd prefer something big and bold without the bother of yearly replanting, then look beyond the cabbage family to some handsome perennial vegetables. In mild climates, artichokes (*Cynara scolymus* and cvs., Zones 8–9) are fantastic as foliage accents, with large, jagged-edged, gray-green to silvery leaves in dense clumps that can easily fill a space 3 to 4 feet across. The plants send up branching stems in summer, with gigantic buds that open into amazing thistlelike, electric blue flowers if you don't pick them.

In cooler regions, consider rhubarb (*Rheum rhabarbarum* and cvs., Zones 3–9) instead. Give it a site with compost-enriched soil, and in a few years, you'll enjoy a splendid show of broad, red-stemmed, bright green leaves in a clump 2 to 3 feet tall and 3 to 4 feet wide. Left alone, mature clumps send up 3-foot-tall stalks that carry plumes of white flowers in summer. Rhubarb might go dormant during the hottest part of summer, unless you plan to mulch heavily and water regularly during dry spells. When temperatures moderate a bit and rainfall is more regular, the clumps will quickly produce fresh leaves and look great until frost. The edible part of rhubarb is its leaf stalks, not the leaves themselves. You can take generous harvests—mostly from early spring to early summer—from clumps that are at least a few years old without interfering with their ornamental value.

ADD COLOR AS WELL AS TASTE

Form and texture aren't the only contributions that vegetable plants make to the ornamental garden: They can provide outstanding color as well.

'Hopi Red Dye' amaranth adds back-of-the-border bang with its red/burgundy color, which follows the theme of the area.

To create a bold focal point, the eye-catching foliage comes from Portuguese kale, not from an exotic ornamental.

For front-of-the-border color, this purple basil provides a color punch that won't quit.

STAY ON TOP OF FOLIAGE PESTS

One of the biggest problems for plants in the cabbage family is caterpillars, who chew large holes in the leaves. Many times, the problem is minor, and you can deal with it by handpicking the pests or snipping off affected leaves; spraying with the biological control agent Bt (*Bacillus thuringiensis* var. *kurstaki*) greatly minimizes the damage. The holes that flea beetles create in the leaves of mustard, bok choy, and eggplant are tinier, but their damage is equally unattractive. They can be difficult to control, but sprays based on spinosad, neem, or capsaicin may help.

Wonderful shapes and colors abound among the lettuces, from the bright chartreuse of 'Australian Yellow' and 'Gold Rush' to the red-speckled green of 'Flashy Trout's Back' (also known as 'Forellenschluss') to the velvety deep red of 'Merlot' and 'Outredgeous'. Beets, too, offer some outstanding dark-leaved varieties, such as 'Bull's Blood' and 'Macgregor's Favorite'. Other ornamental-and-edible options include the ferny-leaved mustards—'Golden Streaks', with yellowish green leaves, and 'Ruby Streaks', with purple leaves—and the broad-leaved bok choy variety 'Violetta', with glossy, nearly black foliage. All of these make great annual alternatives to heucheras for foliage interest.

At the other end of the height spectrum are tall edibles such as orach (*Atriplex hortensis* and cvs., annual), which can reach up to 6 feet tall. 'Golden' orach is greenish yellow; 'Rubra' orach has deep red stems, leaves, and seed heads. Another tall selection for intensely deep red stems, leaves, and seed plumes is 'Hopi Red Dye' amaranth (*Amaranthus cruentus* 'Hopi Red Dye', annual). Both the orachs and the amaranth can provide an ample supply of young leaves for salads without interfering with their border display.

Yet another must-have for luscious leaves is Swiss chard. It grows in 1- to 2-foot-tall fountain-shaped clumps, with bright green or deep red leaves that have contrasting veins and stalks. You can find some single-color strains, such as 'Rhubarb' and 'Charlotte' in red; 'Bright Yellow' in yellow; and 'Fordhook Giant', with bright white stems and veins. But if you really want to make the most of the color range, buy a pack of 'Bright Lights' or 'Five Color' seeds or transplants and select some of each color that appears; a mix usually includes red, orange, yellow, pink, and white.

Showy fruit are the forte of many members of the family Solanaceae, including tomatoes and peppers. Small-fruited cherry tomatoes, as well as the even tinier-fruited currant types, can climb through tuteurs or other decorative supports or scramble up through the stems of shrubby companions, festooning them with small yellow flowers and clusters of red, orange, or yellow rounded or pear-shaped fruit. Tomato plants themselves usually aren't that interesting, but for something really different, seek out 'Variegated', with cream- to white-splashed leaves and medium-size red fruit.

Peppers form low, bushy plants in the range of 1 to 3 feet tall. Their fruit are usually green or deep purple when they first form, ripening to bright shades of red, orange, yellow, or purple, and they range in size and shape from tiny round globes or tapering cones to substantial, blocky, bell-type peppers. Those with the most abundant, most colorful, and most easily visible fruit are the scorchingly hot types, such as the exquisite 'Black Pearl', which also offers deep purple foliage. You can also find, however, equally ornamental selections with easier-to-eat fruit, such as multicolored 'Sweet Pickles'.

Why waste space on plants that are just pretty faces? If you start mixing in some that are both showy and productive, you'll never be at a loss for a side dish or salad fixings. What a great excuse to spend your grocery money on the garden instead.

This colorful combination tastes good too. Pair 'Black Pearl' pepper with 'Australian Yellow' lettuce.

FRONT-YARD
VEGETABLES

Don't be afraid to put your vegetable garden front and center. With a few simple design tips from garden designer Darcy Daniels, you'll be proud to use edibles to add curb appeal.

IT SEEMS LIKE EVERYONE WANTS TO GROW VEGETABLES THESE days, but many homeowners are reluctant to do so in their front yard, even when it happens to be the sunniest, most desirable spot.

After all, vegetable gardens can get chaotic by the end of the growing season, and they tend to look stark and bare in the off-season. But front-yard veggie gardens that have multiseasonal appeal can be created, such as the garden that I designed for Kristan and Ben Sias in Portland, Oregon. Kristan, an avid cook, had been growing edibles in a small, out-of-the-way corner of her front yard for years. The location's size and limited sunlight prevented her from growing the amount and variety of food that she wanted. This new design and location, however, offers plenty of room for edibles—plus a pleasing streetside view.

Easy access is just one of the perks that this front-yard veggie garden has to offer. The side door to the right of the garage leads straight to the kitchen, making it a short commute from garden to table.

THREE STEPS TRANSFORM A BLANK
SLATE INTO A DREAM GARDEN

Moving your veggie garden from the background to the foreground takes some effort. A permanent raised-bed design for a front-yard location requires more planning the first time around than an annual backyard veggie garden. This extra effort and forethought pays off in the long run, however, requiring less labor in the years to come. Follow these three steps to help transform your available front-yard space into an amazing edible garden:

1. PLAN THE LAYOUT

Consider a number of options before landing on a final design. Brainstorm with tissue overlays on a base map—this lets you quickly and freely rough out choices. Once an idea resonates, firm up the preferred concept by fine-tuning the dimensions and determining construction details. Keep in mind that the human eye is able to pick up remarkably small deviations in alignment. Geometric patterns require a bit more rigid planning and a deeper understanding of your site than nongeometric ones.

2. SHAPE THE BEDS

If you decide to incorporate tight curves in your design, you will need to have a fabricator roll (shape) the steel. Don't be dissuaded by this extra step. Steel shapes can be mathematically described and then fabricated in a straightforward process, which shouldn't break the bank if you keep your design relatively simple.

3. CHOOSE THE PLANTS

Edibles that will be on display in your front yard should bring more to the table than just good eating. Think foliage, flowers, and fruit. Attractive foliage is readily available in plants such as kale, rhubarb, artichoke, chard, and lettuce. The flowers of nasturtiums, scarlet runner beans, and espaliered apples provide colorful

blooms, while fruit such as 'Sun Gold' tomatoes, eggplant, peppers (especially red ones), and blueberries provide additional interest.

BEFORE

AFTER

LET THE SPACE INSPIRE THE DESIGN

A front-yard vegetable garden requires as much attention and forethought as a highly visible ornamental garden, especially when space is at a premium. Start planning your layout by considering the shape of your space; employ curves, angles, and straight lines to create an efficient and artful design.

The layout of the Siases' vegetable garden works with the shape of their driveway, which curves along the upper portion. A 20-foot-wide section of yard is available in the front, tapering to a narrow $6^1/2$-foot-wide strip at the rear. A mix of straight lines and curves makes the most of this unique space (see the sidebar at left). The raised beds are laid out in a grid of 5-foot squares modified with curves, resulting in a geometric pattern with pleasing and practical proportions that ground the garden. The geometric grid also instills a sense of order and visual appeal when the garden is overflowing with produce, as well as when it's dormant. An additional interior curve in the central garden space not only lends artistic flair but also enlarges the central intersection, which would otherwise be too narrow and awkward to maneuver within.

When designing a garden layout, plan for adequate pathways and points of access so that you have room to work in the garden. Keep your main pathway at least 3 feet wide to maneuver within—supplemental pathways can be narrower yet still serviceable. Raised beds wider than 4 feet are difficult to work in, but incorporating enough usable pathways to provide access from multiple sides makes tending and harvesting easier.

PICK MATERIALS FOR STYLE AND FUNCTION

Regardless of whether you have inground beds or raised beds, use attractive weatherproof materials to define them. The Siases' garden uses a great material: steel. It is low maintenance, lasts indefinitely, and is space efficient. I also like the warm, earthy tones of rusted steel. The flat-bar steel used in the Siases' garden is only $3/16$ inch thick, making it easy to shape. This allows the design to steer away from straight lines toward graceful curves and more complex geometric shapes. You can opt to create the beds yourself, but because of the complex layout employed in this design, the Siases hired a local contractor to make and install the steel frames. The do-it-yourself route will require you to locate a local industrial-materials supplier or metal fabricator, which may be easier to find if you're located near a major city. You'll also want to call ahead to make sure that the company doesn't operate strictly as a wholesale supplier.

Although steel is great, other materials can be used successfully too. Cedar and composite lumber work well for beds that use straight lines and regular angles. Brick or natural stone can be used to create long-lasting edging that feels organic. A hedge of dwarf boxwood can serve as a living evergreen boundary if you're not using raised beds and are willing to put in a bit more labor to maintain it. Remember, however, to take the thickness of your edging material into consideration. Natural stone or a planted edge will be tricky for small beds because they'll take up a greater percentage of your growing area.

Incorporate art to take your veggie garden from simply functional to ornamental. This locally designed piece is especially useful for adding interest when veggies start to wane.

With the raised-bed or border material chosen, pathway materials come next. The paths of the Siases' garden use compacted gravel to provide all-season access and achieve a neat, crisp appearance that's especially attractive next to the warm tones of rusted metal. The gravel, the steel, and the adjacent driveway all have a tendency to capture and radiate heat, a boon when growing heat-loving veggies such as tomatoes or peppers.

ADD ORNAMENTS THAT HAVE A PURPOSE

Trellises, decorative cages, and garden ornaments provide the finishing touch to a garden. The open central axis of the Siases' garden incorporates a focal point to add interest to the space both during and after the growing season. The Siases commissioned an art-glass piece by two local artists. The glass underscores the garden's unified color theme (created by the combination of materials, structures, and ornaments), which helps ensure that all the details in the garden come together as a whole. A similar artistic display can be achieved in your own garden by incorporating a unifying central focal point, such as a pot, birdbath, fountain, or other decorative element. Working ornamentation, like trellises and cages, saves space and gives your plants support—but they need not be ordinary or eyesores. The Siases' garden uses circular tomato cages made by a local artisan; the cages' rusted-steel texture blends perfectly with the edging of the beds. Aesthetics aside, most support structures need to be easy to move from bed to bed. While the layout and position of your beds are constant, the types of plants grown in them will vary from year to year as you rotate your crops. Many plants will grow on a structure where they're encouraged to twine and climb. The Siases' espaliered apples along their boundary fence are a decorative and space-saving way to incorporate fruit. Because space is tight in many city gardens, growing vertically provides extra room, and the varying heights bring added visual interest to the garden.

Be careful, though, not to overdo it. Too much ornamentation can create chaos and visual clutter. The cohesiveness of the Siases' garden can be at least partly attributed to a disciplined color palette and limited materials. Choose similar themes and stick to them. The results will give you almost as much pleasure as eating your own homegrown fruits and vegetables.

GIVE PLANTINGS A VERTICAL LIFT

Structures add drama and height to the flat plane of the kitchen garden, while also giving you more space to grow colorful and edible climbers. They can be rustic or formal, wood or metal, vibrant or muted. An elegant trellis in the middle of a garden can be stunning—even if it's bare. When left in the garden, brightly painted structures, like this royal blue tuteur, can provide much-needed color on gray winter days. I like to place vertical structures amid seas of foliage that need a focal point. —Jennnifer Bartley

Is this a bold, expensive tropical plant? Nope, it's a broad-leaved squash. It adds a unique form to this beautiful bed, while the garlic chives in back provide a delicious, long-lasting floral display.

✓ CONTAINER GARDENS
✓ DESIGN SOLUTIONS

FINDING SPACE
FOR VEGGIES

All you need to grow your favorite edibles is a sunny place. The best part? The spot can be as small as the corner of a balcony or as big as your backyard. Just follow kitchen-garden designer Sarah Bush's techniques to fit your veggies in anywhere.

LATELY, THERE SEEMS TO BE A LOT OF FARMER ENVY IN THE gardening world. The recent locavore trend, food-contamination scares, and the high price of produce have many grasping the shovel and looking at their lawns with a hungry gleam in their eye. Self-sufficiency and the desire to grow our own food for pleasure and health is appealing, but not all of us have a lawn that we can (or want) to convert into a big vegetable garden. If you work creatively within your means, however, you might find that the joys of a small-space veggie garden far outweigh the expense and hard work of a larger garden. Whether your limited resources include a tiny patch of earth, a sunny driveway or balcony, or the existing landscape around your home, you can use the following techniques to get up close and personal with your food supply. And as a bonus, you'll find that it's much easier to stay on top of weeding, watering, and pest management if your crops are a reasonable size.

RAISED BEDS CAN FIT ANYWHERE

Perhaps you have a sunny patch of ground available, but you don't want to go through the trouble of digging into and amending the hard-packed earth. Or maybe you rent your home, and your landlord doesn't want you digging up the yard. Gardening in a raised bed is a simple way to get the maximum yield from a small area without having to disturb the soil beneath. I like to think of a raised bed as my own personal salad bar, which can fit just about anywhere—as long as it's in full sun.

But what if the only place you have plenty of sun is your driveway? No problem. You can build a raised bed on top of concrete or asphalt. The key is to create a barrier between the impervious surface and the soil that your veggies are growing in to provide proper drainage, block contaminants, and keep your plants from cooking on the hot surface. Shovel a layer of wood chips several inches thick onto an area 2 feet wider and longer than your raised bed. Keep the chips in place by edging the area with bricks or stones. Center the box accordingly, then place a layer of cardboard along the bottom to keep the soil from washing out and to prevent asphalt oils from coming in contact with the soil. Then, fill the bed with soil that is free of weed seeds.

I used this technique last year to build one of my signature salad-bar gardens on top of a thin parking strip alongside a sidewalk. To construct the bed, I used 8-inch-wide rot-resistant cedar planks. I avoid using pressure-treated wood because it contains chemicals that can leach into the soil. I stacked two of the boards on top of each other to create a depth of 16 inches. The deeper the bed, the more room plants have to spread out their root systems (leading to better health) and the less watering you'll have to do. I made my box sturdy by attaching 2×2 posts to each corner.

You can make your bed as long and as wide as your space can accommodate. Mine ended up being 6 feet long and 4 feet wide. Keep in mind that the bed should be narrow enough so that you can comfortably reach into the center from either side. This allows you to tend your garden without stepping into it and compacting the soil. In this one small bed, I planted a wide array of veggies, herbs, and edible flowers—enough to make a luscious and vibrant salad for lunch or dinner on a daily basis (see the sidebar on the facing page).

And remember, containers are just another form of a raised bed. Depending on how much or how little space you've got, you can use traditional clay pots, wooden fruit crates, galvanized-steel garbage cans, or plastic buckets—anything that holds soil will work as long as you can drill holes in the bottom.

THE KEY TO SUCCESS IS INTENSIVE PLANTING

To get the biggest possible harvest from your containers and small raised beds, you need to ignore traditional spacing requirements. Don't get me wrong: I still allow room for my plants to grow, but I often read what the plant label says and cut it in half. Spacing requirements are usually based on traditional, inground gardens consisting of long, single rows spaced at least 3 feet apart so that farmers can navigate machinery up and down the rows. An intensively planted garden keeps wasted space to a minimum. Also, crops that are continually harvested—for example, lettuce, chard, and herbs—are always being pruned and rarely reach their full-grown size, so they can be placed close together. Placing your plants closer to each other also crowds out weeds and protects your soil from the drying effects of the sun and wind.

At the center or rear of your container or raised bed, plant things that like to climb—such as tomatoes, cucumbers, and peas—to save space and to keep fruit off the ground. Even vines with heavy fruit, like squash or melons, can be trained upward on a bamboo teepee or railing.

A bright orange oil-drum container can find the perfect home on a balcony or in a back alley while providing summer melons for snacking.

THE SALAD-BAR GARDEN

A small bed, like this 6-foot-long and 4-foot-wide garden, can produce enough fresh produce for a daily salad. Harvesting starts in early spring and continues through fall.

1 Sunflowers (six plants) Tall sunflowers, with their edible seeds and petals, provide needed shade to the salad greens below. Trellised indeterminate tomatoes could also be used.

2 Swiss chard (nine plants) This is a good source of summer greens. Chard lasts longer than lettuce and keeps producing well into fall. The bright stems hold their color when cooked.

3 Strawberries (four plants) A few strawberry plants go a long way after producing runners, which cascade over the edges of the bed. By the second year, these few plants will produce several pints of berries.

4 Thyme (four plants) Because it is a drought-tolerant plant, thyme does well as a filler between the aggressive, thirsty strawberry plants. Use it fresh in salads for a pungent snap, or cooked with fish or poultry.

5 Marigolds (four plants) The flowers taste like lemon and tolerate hot conditions and low amounts of water—perfect for a sidewalk raised bed.

6 Curly parsley (two plants) This herb forms small, mounded tufts, which are the perfect shape to round out the sharp back corners of the bed. It's an excellent green to add to a salad.

THE BEST CONTAINER VEGETABLES

There are so many great vegetables that can be grown in containers. Here are just a few of my favorites.

1- TO 2-GALLON POTS
• 'Touchon' carrots
• 'Evergreen White Bunching' scallions
• Shallots
• Garlic

3-GALLON POTS
• 'Tom Thumb' lettuce
• 'Golden' beets
• 'Cherry Belle' radishes
• Mustard greens
• 'Tokyo Cross' turnips

5-GALLON POTS
• 'Tiny Tim' cherry tomatoes
• 'Salad Bush' cucumbers
• 'Little Fingers' eggplant
• 'Miniature Red Bell' peppers
• 'Sugar Baby' watermelon

25-GALLON POTS
• Burpee's 'Fourth of July' potato collection
• 'Oregon Spring' tomatoes
• 'Table Gold' winter squash
• 'Tom Thumb' popcorn

—Sylvia Thompson

Even a formal ornamental garden can be spruced up when given an edible bean trellis as a focal point.

Use sections of panty hose or old dish towels, and make little hammocks to support the fruit as it grows.

To save even more room, sprinkle some lettuce, spinach, or arugula seeds around the base of tall edibles like dill, fennel, peppers, and eggplant. The greens will sprout quickly and thrive in the shade produced by their taller neighbors when the weather gets hot. Creepers—like strawberries, tomatillos, thyme, and nasturtium—make good perimeter plants because they take up minimal amounts of space by cascading over the sides of containers and beds.

EMBED EDIBLES WITH ORNAMENTALS

If you're not sure you want to commit to maintaining raised beds or containerized veggies, you can incorporate edibles into the existing landscape around your home. Many edibles with notable colors, textures, or forms can be used in place of ornamentals.

Ornamental gardens often lack vertical accents. To add a tall twist to an otherwise flat garden, I like to build teepees and grow a variety of beans or peas on them (see the photo above). Many members of the legume family have not only delicious edible pods but also beautiful flowers and lush foliage. Unless your garden contains tropical foliage, you are probably in need of some plants with bold forms as well. I like to mix in some broad-leaved squash (see the photo on p. 60) in ornamental gardens to add impact. And when it comes to texture, I love to tuck in the puckered leaves of lacinato kale or the fuzzy fronds of artichokes. Red or rainbow chard has a cool texture as well as vibrant coloring (see the photo below). My other favorite plants to use for their standout hues are 'Red Sails' lettuce and purple basil. Why plant green when you can have the same great taste with a brighter-colored option?

Remember that the blooms of many herbs last longer and are more eye-catching than many ornamentals. Onions and garlic chives display globes of tiny blossoms in spring that rival any ornamental allium in beauty (see the photo on p. 60). Hardy herbs—such as rosemary, sage, and lavender—can easily take the place of evergreens in warm zones, whereas thyme and wintergreen (*Gaultheria procumbens*, USDA Hardiness Zones 3–8) make fragrant and delicious ground covers. But my favorite edible addition to existing landscapes are blueberries: Replace any deciduous shrub with a blueberry bush for beautiful fall foliage and pretty white flowers in spring; the delicious berries are a bonus. With so many different options, there's no reason (or excuse) not to find space for at least a few vegetables. With a bit of creativity and some effort, you can have access to fresh, mouthwatering food for much of the year—something an ornamental grass can never provide.

No matter how little land you've got, there's always room for vegetables. A tiny roadside raised bed stops traffic and provides plenty of fresh produce.

CREATE THE PERFECT VEGGIE PARTNERSHIP

Certain vegetables, when planted together, can help each other out. One of the most famous partnerships, called "the Three Sisters," groups beans, corn, and squash together. But there are numerous other beneficial partnerships in the veggie world, as well as some bad pairings to avoid.

GOOD PAIRINGS

Asparagus and parsley. Parsley repels the dreaded asparagus beetle.

Nasturtium and squash. Nasturtium repels squash bugs.

Eggplant and lima beans. Lima beans deter the Colorado potato beetle, which destroys eggplants.

BAD PAIRINGS

Tomatoes and potatoes. Both are prone to blight and often infect each other with the disease.

Corn and tomatoes. They attract the harmful tomato hornworm and corn earworm, which destroy fruit.

Cabbage and lettuce or strawberries. Cabbage competes for the same nutrients as lettuce and strawberries.

Get gobs of fruit from only 84 square feet. This small space can produce a bigger harvest than plots twice its size thanks to some tried-and-true techniques.

BIGGER YIELDS
FROM SMALL GARDENS

Living in a grower's paradise, master gardener Peter Garnham has devised a system that allowed him to grow high-yielding edible plants in his small space. Well-timed transplants and inventive trellising helped create a continuous harvest throughout the growing season.

I HAVE LIVED—AND GARDENED—IN THREE COUNTRIES: England, Barbados, and the United States. In the United States, I found myself settled on the eastern tip of New York's Long Island, a grower's paradise in USDA Hardiness Zone 7. Deep, rich soils combined with a long growing season—and a ready market from local stores and restaurants—persuaded me to start growing commercial crops. A local nursery owner let me cultivate an unused portion of his leased land, which enabled me to set up dozens of 4-foot-wide by 200-foot-long beds in the incredible 11-foot-deep topsoil. It was there that I learned the advantages of drip irrigation and the disadvantages of white-tailed deer.

Perhaps as a reaction to the burden of that intensively planted 5 acres, my home garden is small. It is 14 feet wide by 36 feet long, a fenced rectangle of soil that I created from compost and green manures. Unlike the market garden, my home garden is built on sand that has a bare inch of topsoil. After 10 years of adding amendments, the soil was about where I wanted it: a pH of 6.5 and an organic content of 5 percent. Still sandy, it drains well.

Seed-starting tools are crucial. Soil blocks (right) and indoor lights (below) enable gardeners to grow lots of high-quality transplants in a small space.

Soil blocks fit neatly into flats and cold frames. The flats are three-sided wooden frames that have an open side to allow for drainage (left). Flats filled with mature seedlings are placed in a cold frame for hardening off (below).

With a market garden, tending it full time is what you do. But my home garden has to take its turn with the other priorities in my life, such as earning a living, running a small museum, volunteering as an emergency medical technician, and talking about gardening to garden clubs and extension classes. It is essential, therefore, that I have things sufficiently well organized so that the garden never gets away from me.

TRANSPLANTS ARE THE KEY TO CONTINUOUS PRODUCTION

Like most gardeners, I suffer from late-winter catalog fever. I always buy too many seeds of more varieties than I can possibly grow. I can't help it: I'm an addict. But thanks to indoor planting, most of my plants eventually find a home. All my early plantings are transplants that I start inside under lights. There is no better cure for the winter blahs than a roomful of seedlings. I've attached fluorescent fixtures (cheap bright-white tubes, not the expensive warm-white or wide-spectrum grow lights) to plywood boards and suspended the boards by chains from tall sawhorses. The chains allow me to raise the lights as seedlings get taller.

My preference is for 2-inch-square soil cubes rather than plastic pots or trays. Roots reach the edge of the soil block and stop; they don't circle around, as they can with pots. With soil blocks, transplant shock is negligible or nonexistent. I use an organic soil mix. Mixed with water, it forms soil cubes that hold together, and it contains enough compost to eliminate the need for supplemental feeding. I place the blocks in flats made out of plywood and 1×2 lumber. The flats have three sides, with the fourth side left open to allow for drainage. I bottom-water by placing the flats in a large plastic pan containing about 3 inches of water. This keeps the leaves dry—an important way to avoid fungal diseases. After the soil cubes have absorbed enough water, I let the excess drain off.

I move the seedlings out into two cold frames as soon as daytime temperatures permit. One cold frame is in a shady spot; the other has old screen windows (with shade cloth replacing the screening) laid across the top to allow the seedlings to harden off gently. In early spring, this means carrying a lot of flats out in the morning and back in at night, but it is a small price to pay for inexpensive and healthy transplants.

ABOVE Access is important, even in a tight space. Paths of 2×10 lumber enable the author to harvest his crops without trampling the plants. The planks also secure essential drip-irrigation lines.

RIGHT Don't leave blank spaces empty for long. As early-spring crops peak and begin to decline, they should be removed to make way for a crop of late-season transplants.

Once the seedlings are hardened off, the soil cubes are easily transplanted into the garden. My three-finger-scoop method beats any tool I have found: Plunge three fingers into the soil, pull the soil back, and plop the soil cube into the space created. Fluff a little soil over the top of the cube (to prevent moisture from wicking out), firm the soil around it, and move on to the next spot. When I've finished, I water everything in to remove any trapped air.

Transplants are essential to start the season early and to provide some succession plantings. I start first with up to 10 varieties of lettuce, three or four varieties each of tomatoes and peppers, and long-season crops, like leeks. The lettuces and leeks go out to cold frames early on, while tomatoes and peppers stay indoors under the warmth of the lights. This leaves room indoors for flats of herbs and several flowers. In late summer, I start winter crops—like cabbage, broccoli, and kale—and a final round of lettuce. By starting the fall lettuce inside under lights, the seedlings avoid the worst summer heat (some lettuces won't even germinate in hot soil, and many more

just bolt), and they are ready to transplant when the weather cools off a bit.

At the same time that early transplants go out into the garden, I direct-sow many salad crops for cut-and-come-again use. When the transplants have matured and been harvested, I replace them with later transplants, such as parsley, basil, sage, and thyme. I direct-sow peas and beans, then tear them out and replace them in mid- to late summer when they pass their peak, which gives me room for a fall crop.

STRUCTURES INCREASE SPACE EFFICIENCY

I place 4-foot-long 2×10 planks across the garden and longer pieces to run end to end. These serve as walkways and enclose the 4-foot-square beds. I flip them over occasionally to expose pests, such as slugs and sow bugs, and to counteract cupping of the boards. My drip-irrigation lines run under the planks, which do not, as you might expect, interfere with the flow of water. In late December, I remove all the planks and store them, with narrow strips of wood between them to allow for air circulation.

I am convinced that drip irrigation is the only way to water a garden. In addition to putting water where plants need it and keeping it off the leaves, it is also economical—there's almost no loss of water to evaporation. With a small fertilizer injector connected to the system, I can feed a little fish-seaweed fertilizer down the lines when needed. My hose layout is permanent; I drag it out of the way only in early spring to cultivate the whole garden, then I replace it. The lines have emitters every foot and are spaced about 2 feet apart.

Four kinds of plants need support: squash, beans, peas, and tomatoes. All four get the same basic treatment to increase their production and to help me gain a bit more space. I hammer 8-foot-long 2×2 poles 2 feet into the ground, about 6 feet apart along the row. I then drive two nails, about ¹/₂ inch apart, into the tops of the poles. Eight-foot lengths of steel rebar rest between these nails (see the right photo below). Their weight holds them in place, and they form the top support.

Squash, peas, and beans climb 6-inch-square nylon netting suspended from the rebar and stapled to the poles.

For tomatoes, I tie biodegradable garden twine around the base of the plant, wind it around the stem, and secure it to the rebar overhead. As the tomato plant grows, I keep twirling the plant around the twine; I find that attending to this task once a week is enough. I prune off all side shoots, which allows me to plant tomatoes at 16-inch spacing. As the plants mature, I remove all lower leaves so that none touches the ground, minimizing the transference of soil-borne diseases.

Tunnels of floating row-cover fabric (supported on wire hoops) are my principal protection against insects. The only pesticide I use is Bt (*Bacillus thuringiensis*) against caterpillars. If you discover the life cycle of insect enemies, then you will know when to install and remove covers. The best way to acquire this knowledge is by observation and record keeping. All my techniques might sound like a lot of work, but if you analyze them, you will see that they are, in fact, the reverse. I take time in the off-season—December through February—to set up equipment, order seeds, and prepare record sheets. Throughout the growing season, my garden gets attention when I can spare it from my other activities. Like most living creatures, it seems to do well with what one observer describes as "benevolent neglect."

This trellis is simple yet versatile. For tomatoes, twine is wound around the stems of the plants and secured above to the rebar pole (left). This trellis is made out of 2×2 wooden stakes and lengths of steel rebar, which are cradled at the top of the stakes between two nails (below).

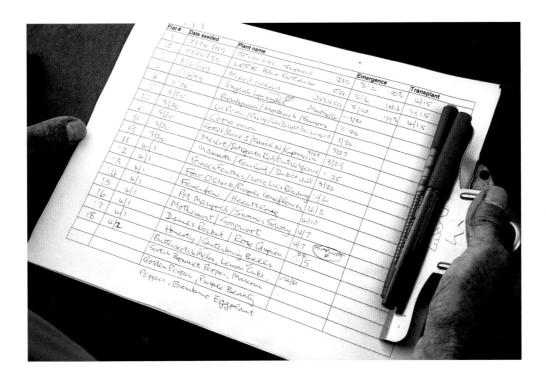

THE VIRTUES OF RECORD KEEPING

For tracking seed starts, I create record sheets on my computer and then fill them in by hand (see the photo above). They contain the seed-flat number (I paint numbers on all my flats with cotton-swab "paintbrushes"), the date something is seeded, the plant name, the date it emerged, and the hardening-off (cold frame) and transplant dates.

GET THE TIMING RIGHT

Recording the data takes seconds, and I have an invaluable guide for the following year. A brief note such as "Start two weeks later!" reminds me not to be so eager to seed tomatoes the following year. These notes help me rearrange seeding times so that slow starters, such as leeks, are started early enough to coincide with ideal transplant dates, and they also encourage me to plant more or less of some things. At the end of the year, I staple the sheets together for winter reading.

REMEMBER WHAT WENT WHERE

I have a frequently updated record sheet for the garden too. A simple tic-tac-toe diagram, it shows what was planted in which bed, when it was planted, and whether it was a transplant or was direct-sown. This record allows me to rotate crops so that I don't plant the same thing in the same place two years running. When an insect pest appears, I note the date. I also keep a yearly list of seed varieties that I have bought, the year they were purchased, and sources, with notes about how well—or how poorly—a plant did. This is enough to keep me from wasting time planting three-year-old onion seeds, and it reminds me that seeds from a particular source, or of a certain variety, are not good performers.

Raised beds can go where no other garden can. Whether you're trying to avoid your preexisting soil or your sunniest spot happens to be on a hill, a raised bed is the perfect solution. A few rocks along the bottom help level the bed at this site.

✓ HOW-TO

✓ LOW-MAINTENANCE
   IDEAS

✓ ECO-FRIENDLY OPTION

BUILDING
RAISED BEDS

When landscape designer Linda Chisari moved into her Southern California home, she was faced with a number of land challenges that could have made growing edibles difficult. Rather than give up, she built raised beds, which allowed her to grow more food from better soil using less water. She shares how to build a raised bed in order to create a better home for your veggies.

RAISED BEDS SOLVED MANY OF THE GARDEN PROBLEMS THAT faced me 20 years ago in our new home. Among the challenges were terrible soil, a concrete-paved yard, arid growing conditions, small children, and a big, exuberant puppy. When we read the real estate agent's description of our house-to-be, four words eclipsed all others: "perfect backyard for pool." To me, those words meant a warm southern exposure and a sizable empty space in which to plant a vegetable garden.

The sizable sunny space turned out to be about 2,000 square feet of concrete pavement. True, it was large enough for a decent-size garden. But also true was that what little soil existed was heavily compacted and lacked organic content. Once before, we had been faced with difficult growing conditions. On a granite ledge with no soil in New Hampshire, my husband had built a raised bed where I grew a small salad garden. So I figured, why not design a system of raised beds that would allow me to grow vegetables at this new home?

DECIDE ON THE MATERIALS AND A DESIGN

There were a number of reasons why raised beds seemed the perfect way to garden. First, my husband was an accomplished carpenter and could build the boxes. Second, we could leave the concrete in place and simply break up the portions under the boxes to provide drainage. Soil quality was a third reason. We were able to fill the beds with soil by using compost from our own pile and supplementing it with some topsoil and chicken manure. This created a great growing medium.

Because we live in a Mediterranean-type climate with less than 10 inches of rainfall per year and almost none between April and November, we knew we would have to irrigate. Raised beds allowed us to set up an irrigation system that included a hose bib in each box. This would allow us to water each bed independently.

USE SCREWS FOR LONG-LASTING BEDS

Nails are fine to use in areas of the country where there is not a lot of rainfall. But wood swells when it's wet, so if you live in a place that gets consistent moisture, use galvanized decking screws to hold your bed together. Remember to predrill the holes first.

Measure, mark, and cut the side posts. You'll need only one 8-foot-long 4×4 post for each bed because you'll cut it into four equal pieces, one for each corner (left). Attach three 8-foot-long 2×6s to the corner posts with nails (right).

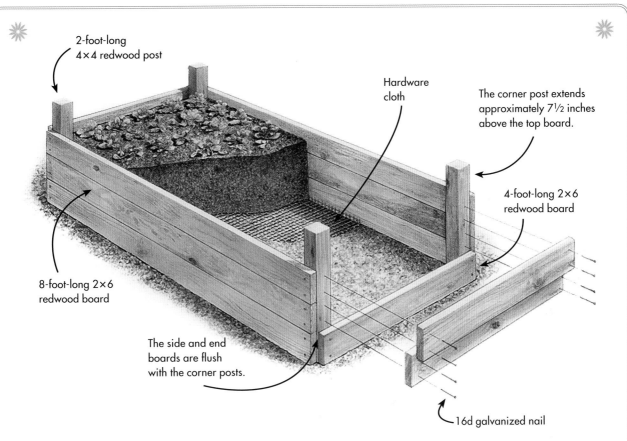

2-foot-long 4×4 redwood post

Hardware cloth

The corner post extends approximately 7½ inches above the top board.

4-foot-long 2×6 redwood board

8-foot-long 2×6 redwood board

The side and end boards are flush with the corner posts.

16d galvanized nail

THE BLUEPRINT FOR A RAISED BED

1 To make the corner posts, measure and cut the 8-foot-long 4×4 into four 2-foot lengths.

2 To make the long sides of the bed, nail three 8-foot-long 2×6s one at a time to two corner posts; you will have boards stacked three high. The bottom board should be flush with the bottom of the post, while the top board should end approximately 7½ inches short of the top of the post. Repeat to form the second long side.

3 Cut the remaining three 2×6s in half so that you have six 4-foot-long 2×6s for the short ends.

4 Stand the two long sides of the bed parallel to each other, approximately 4 feet apart. Nail the 2×6 end pieces to the corner posts, three to each end. Align them so that they are flush with the posts. The raised-bed form is now complete.

5 If you're worried about gophers or moles, staple an 8-foot-long by 4-foot-wide piece of ½-inch-square hardware cloth across the bottom of the box. This allows drainage and root growth but keeps the critters out.

WHAT YOU'LL NEED (PER BED)

- One 8-foot-long 4×4 redwood post for the corners
- Nine 8-foot-long 2×6 redwood boards for sides and ends
- One 1-pound box of 16d (3½-inch-long) galvanized nails
- ½-inch-square hardware cloth, 8 feet long by 4 feet wide

AVOID BLACK WALNUT TREES

The biggest problem I have seen recently with raised beds is with black walnut trees (*Juglans nigra*, USDA Hardiness Zones 5–9). Growing plants, such as tomatoes, near a black walnut tree is a recipe for disaster because this tree secretes certain chemicals that are poisonous to other plants. Gardeners might think they could use a raised bed to avoid this problem; unfortunately, this only works for about a year, because the tree's roots will grow into the raised bed and its leaves will fall onto it. In short, don't place your raised beds near black walnut trees.

—Jeff Gillman

Pull it all together. Stand up the constructed long sides of the bed so that they are 4 feet apart and parallel to each other. Complete the bed by nailing the short 4-foot-long 2×6 boards to the posts.

It didn't take long for us to see that our raised beds had several unanticipated advantages. Our golden retriever loved to race around the beds but rarely jumped into them. Our children could easily ride their Big Wheels® around the obstacle course we had unwittingly developed for them. And neither of these activities nor my gardening compacted the soil because no one ever walked on it. It remained fluffy and well-aerated, allowing plant roots to grow freely.

I wanted eight raised beds, and I wanted them made out of wood. Construction-grade redwood, which contains knots and some imperfections, seemed like a logical choice because we knew it would last many years and would cost less than many other types of wood.

The design of the beds was based on practical considerations. The dimensions, 8 feet long by 4 feet wide, were derived from the fact that lumber is available in 8-foot lengths, so there would be minimal cutting and no waste. I could comfortably reach only 2 feet into the beds, so a width of 4 feet would allow access to the middle of the beds from either side.

I measured several of our chairs and found that they all had a seat height of 16 to 19 inches. Because we had decided to use 2×6 redwood, we could stack the boards three high and end up with a finished height of $16^{1}/_{2}$ inches (the actual width of a 2×6 is $5^{1}/_{2}$ inches). This made the edge of the box a comfortable height on which to perch and gave more than enough root space for the plants.

The boards were nailed to 4×4 corner posts that extend nearly 8 inches higher than the sides. I sometimes drape bird netting for pest protection or row covers for warmth over the posts. The paths between the beds are 3 feet wide to accommodate a wheelbarrow.

ACCESSORIZE YOUR BED

Beds can be customized to meet specific needs. For some clients, I've designed beds that have a 6-inch-wide board or "cap" around the edge to make sitting more comfortable. (This makes it more difficult, however, to turn the soil.) For other beds, I've extended the corner posts up to 8 feet to allow the attachment of trellises for beans, cucumbers, and other climbers. In gopher-prone areas, I've designed beds that have hardware cloth tacked across the bottom. For some beds, I've devised a system of hoops, using PVC irrigation pipe, over which to drape bird netting or row covers to keep cabbage loopers out.

I have experimented with several irrigation products, including microemitters, soaker hoses, and drip pipe. I prefer the flexible soaker hoses available in most hardware and garden stores. They can be snaked in any configuration and are easily removed when it's time to turn the soil. I use inexpensive chopsticks to keep the hoses in place.

Because the price of redwood has risen, many clients ask about using less expensive pressure-treated wood (see the sidebar at right). I discourage them from making this choice because I'm not comfortable using chemically treated products around food crops.

It has been 20 years since we built our beds, and we are beginning to see signs of wear that indicate we need to start rebuilding. They have certainly been a good value, having held up to blasting sun and year-round cultivation. Where there was once only concrete, the soil is now black and rich and teeming with earthworms. The eight beds also make crop rotation easy to track. Everything I've grown in the garden has thrived.

Over the years, we have slowly removed the concrete paving between the boxes and replaced it with a thick layer of pea gravel, which allows the little rain we get to percolate into the ground. And it crunches delightfully underfoot. Because the vegetable garden is the primary view from our kitchen, it has been an added pleasure to look out on the raised beds with their profusion of vegetables, herbs, and edible flowers spilling over the edges. Thanks to the raised beds, we can enjoy homegrown produce every month of the year.

Plastics

Redwood

Red cedar

Cypress

PRESSURE-TREATED ALTERNATIVES

If you'd like to avoid using wood treated with chemical preservatives for your raised beds, here are a couple of options:

RECYCLED-PLASTIC LUMBER

Many of the plastic milk bottles, detergent containers, and grocery bags we recycle are being mixed with wood fiber to make a new generation of decking material: composite lumber. This recycled-plastic lumber is now available in many home-improvement stores.

NATURALLY ROT-RESISTANT WOODS

Redwood, cypress, and red cedar are all, to varying degrees, rot resistant. They can be expensive, though, and supplies may be limited by region.

BAMBOO TRELLIS PLAN

T he number of vines on my garden wish list will soon outnumber the structures on which I can grow them. Is that a bad thing, you ask? It would be if I had to rely on the vine supports for sale at local nurseries and home stores. What I found on a recent shopping trip was either over-priced, lacking in character, or made with flimsy materials. That's what motivated me to make my own trellises out of bamboo.

Bamboo is a wonderfully versa-tile building material and one of the world's most renewable resources. It's lightweight, strong, and flexible, and it looks at home in most garden-ing schemes, even in the garden that surrounds my late-19th-century in-town house. Another plus is that bamboo can last for 8 to 10 years before showing signs of deterioration.

One of the benefits of design-ing and building my own trellises is that I can determine their size. Furthermore, I can work with two cane widths to give my designs more visual interest. To tie the bamboo together, I use a wax-coated black lashing cord that contrasts nicely with the buff-colored bamboo. I mail-order bamboo in bulk to save money and to have extra on hand for other projects. With an invest-ment of less than two hours and for about $10, I have a custom-made trellis for one of the vines in my growing collection.

Create a design. Imagine your trellis where it will eventually be placed, taking into account the size and shape of the area where it will be situated. Draw the design of your trellis on paper. Deciding on as many measurements as possible in advance will help you to stay on track during the building process.

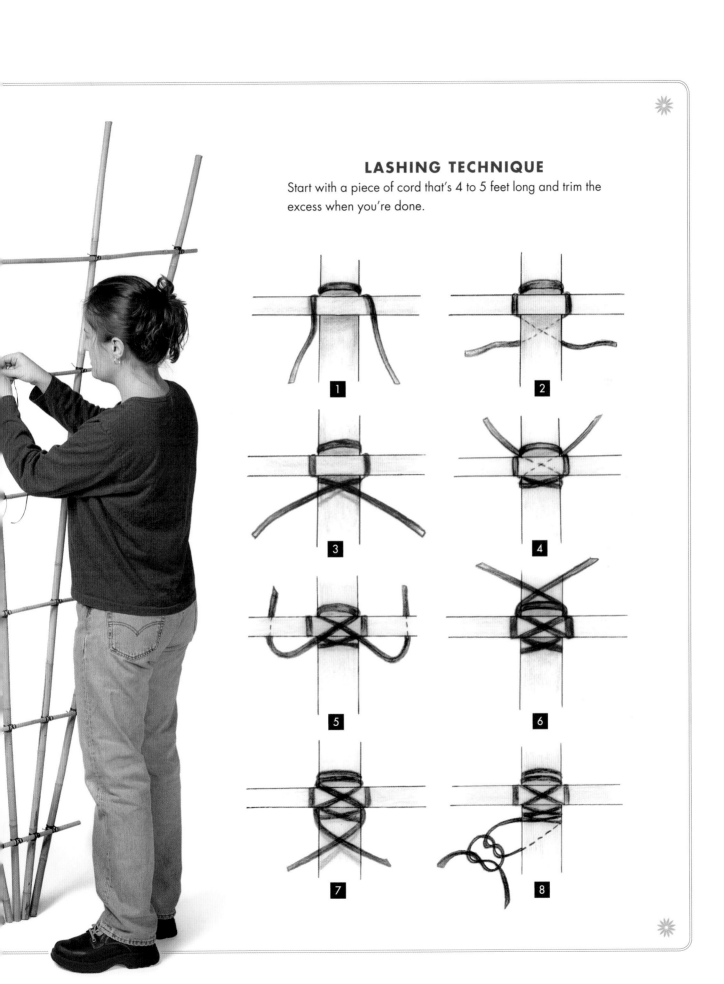

LASHING TECHNIQUE

Start with a piece of cord that's 4 to 5 feet long and trim the excess when you're done.

Many chiles will grow happily in pots. Shown here, clockwise from center back, are 'Fresno', 'Orange Blossom', 'Magenta', 'Hot Claw', and 'Royal Black'.

✓ CONTAINER GARDEN
✓ LOW-MAINTENANCE
  IDEAS
✓ HOW-TO

PERFECT PEPPERS
FOR POTS

Peppers are a gorgeous and delicious addition to any garden, and as gardening author Amy Goldman learned, their beauty can easily be brought indoors at season's end. She shares how digging them up and growing them in containers inside allows you to enjoy an extra harvest in the spring.

ONE FALL SEVERAL YEARS AGO, FACED WITH AN IMPENDING frost, I hastily dug up and potted some of my favorite chile peppers. My peppers quickly revived from being dug up and moved inside, and I've kept them in pots ever since, putting them outside in the summer and bringing them into the greenhouse each fall, essentially treating them as tender perennials instead of annuals. For this, they typically reward me with chiles twice a year, once in May and again in late summer.

The peppers I grow in pots are not exposed to the inclement weather and killing frosts that strike down their garden-bound brethren. During the summer, I can meet their needs for nutrients, light, and water more easily than I can for those in the ground, and they suffer less from soil-borne diseases. However, the main disadvantage to pot culture is that the plants yield less fruit.

GIVE CHILES A SEASON IN THE GROUND

I never start my peppers off in pots; instead, I start plants from seed and transplant them directly into the garden. I don't direct-seed peppers into the garden, either, because they would yield later and produce fewer peppers. If you are unable to start your own seeds, you can purchase transplants at garden centers. Spending its first growing season in the ground rather than in a pot increases a plant's vigor. Toward the end of summer, I choose my favorite plants, usually those with the best silhouettes. I trim them if they need it and spritz them with water to remove any hitchhiking pests. Then I water the ground

Prune peppers back hard in late winter to encourage new, healthy growth.

thoroughly and dig up the plants. I gently remove excess soil and give them a light root pruning.

I move my peppers into terra-cotta or glazed clay pots. I usually use light-colored pots because they reflect the sun, so the soil doesn't dry out as quickly. I use potting soil with additional perlite, vermiculite, or sand, and I also add a slow-release organic fertilizer to the mix. I water the plants well and move them to a shady spot so they can recover.

CHILES LIKE HEAT AND LIGHT

Inside, I try to provide my potted peppers with the kind of growing conditions they would have in their native habitat. They prefer a temperature between 60°F and 75°F and a generous amount of light, which can be supplied by grow lights if necessary. Good drainage, low humidity, and adequate air circulation are also important.

Often, in late winter, my potted chiles drop their leaves and go into dormancy. When the foliage falls, I give the plants a radical pruning, which reinvigorates their growth. First, I remove the hollow and dead stems, then the weak stems, and finally the minor and crossed shoots. Aiming for a structure with an open center and architecture like a deer's antlers, I leave multiple strong stems that I cut back to just above a bud. The plants quickly begin to produce foliage and will often flower and fruit in April and May. When the weather warms up, I move them outside and have another crop of chiles in August and September.

PICK A PEPPER

The best peppers for pots have a compact habit, attractive foliage, and an abundance of small, colorful fruits. These ornamental types often lack the subtle flavors (for example, sweet, chocolaty, fruity, or smoky), but not the fire, of larger-podded types. I find it best to grow the big boys in the open field, since they perform poorly in pots. Here are a few of my favorite chiles for ornamental use.

'Bouquet'

'Fresno'

'Orange Blossom'

'Poinsettia'

'Bouquet'—Purple flowers and foliage with purple fruits that eventually turn red.

'Chinese Multicolor' (syn. 'Joe McCarthy')—Lovely cone-shaped pods of many colors on a large plant.

'Color Guard'—Medium-size lush plant with upright, tapered fruits that turn from orange to purple to red.

'Fips' (syn. 'Fiesta')—Dwarf pepper with clusters of colorful fruits.

'Fresno'—A medium-hot pepper with 3-inch-long fruits.

'Goat Horn'—A cayenne pepper with long (4- to 5-inch) pods.

'Marbles'— 1-foot-high plant with colorful marble-size red fruits.

'Orange Blossom'—Short, bushy plant covered with striking orange erect peppers.

'Nosegay'—Diminutive 6-inch plants loaded with small, colorful, round fruits.

'Poinsettia'—Clusters of upright 3-inch red peppers borne on compact plants.

'Riot'—Short, bushy plant covered with clusters of striking yellow elongated pods that eventually turn red.

'Rojo Morado'—Tall, elegant plant with purple flowers and fruits that eventually turn red.

'Royal Black'—Tall plant notable for its purple and white variegated foliage. Small fruits turn from purple to red at maturity.

It's the first veggie you plant and the first to produce. Peas can be sown in the ground in early spring, and you usually can start harvesting them 55 to 60 days later.

SMALL PEAS
FOR SMALL SPACES

Easy-to-manage dwarf varieties of peas produce more pods than tall vines, so you can fit them in, even in a small garden. Gardener Ron Clancy shares his planting tips to start your peas off right.

REMEMBER CANNED PEAS? IF YOU GREW UP IN THE 1950S, YOU probably do. At that time, there were two ways to get your peas: canned or fresh picked. Today most people get peas from the frozen-food section of a supermarket. But to experience the truly sublime taste of sweet peas, you need to grow your own, then pick them, shell them, and cook them as quickly as possible. Then again, freshly picked peas are so tempting that many of mine never make it from the garden to the kitchen.

I've been growing peas as long as I've been gardening—more than 40 years. At first, the yields were often disappointing, and some years, the harvest season was very short. Many garden books had sketchy or conflicting information on growing peas. Then along came PBS with the first episodes of *Crockett's Victory Garden*. I used some of the tricks Jim Crockett suggested, and added a few of my own, and I was able to increase yields and extend the season of this special crop.

The shelling peas sold in catalogs vary from bush varieties as low as 18 inches to giant vines that reach more than 6 feet long. The dwarf varieties are the most manageable for the home

gardener and produce more per square foot. When selecting varieties, first look for seeds suited to your area, then look at vine length.

PLANT PEAS WHEN THE FORSYTHIA BLOOMS

Common wisdom says that peas should be planted as soon as the ground can be worked. While it is true that peas will germinate in temperatures as low as 40°F, it can take weeks; raise the temperature to 60°F, and germination will occur in nine days. I have found that a happy medium is the best choice. I garden in the Pacific Northwest, where you can sometimes work the soil as early as January; however, I've had the best results planting my first crop of peas when the forsythia just starts to bloom, which here is around the third week of March. I follow this sowing with successive plantings every two to three weeks.

Peas do best in cool weather. Once summer sets in, peas stop producing. During long, cool springs, peas grow well and most years can be harvested into July. Although peas are mainly a spring crop, if you live in an area that usually has a long, warm autumn, you can try planting a fall crop 60 to 90 days before your hard frost date and enjoy fresh peas late into the year.

In the South, gardeners usually plant peas in the fall and grow them as a winter crop. If your fall is cool and damp, viruses will often get the best of any autumnal sowing. You'll have more success growing them in spring and early summer.

Sow seeds thickly. If you plan to grow your peas in a block or trench system, sow the seeds close together so that the emerging vines will help support each other.

Because peas are legumes, which convert atmospheric nitrogen into nitrogen compounds in the soil, they don't need much fertilizer. They will benefit, though, from a light, neutral soil with added organic material. If you want to enhance their nitrogen fixing, coat seeds prior to planting with a pea inoculant, a natural bacterial powder that you can find at most garden centers.

KEEP THE SOIL MOIST AND THE PODS PICKED

Once you have chosen your type of support (see the sidebar on p. 88) and sown your crop, keep the bed watered. In sandy soil, like mine, all it takes is a couple of windy, warm spring days to dry out the soil enough so that the seeds don't properly germinate. Peas need water the most at this point, when they are sprouting, and again when they are blooming.

Once you see the vines blooming, check the plants daily. Pods form quickly, and you want to pick them just as the peas have filled out the shells but before they start getting too mature and starchy. Pick them when they are bright green, full-size, and still sweet. Keeping pods picked also extends the pea season.

A few pests and diseases can keep you from enjoying this idyllic scene. If you find birds attracted to your newly sprouted peas, throw some netting over the plants until they are a couple of inches tall. Another early spring pest is the pea weevil. It notches the leaves but generally disappears after the vines are up a few inches; the peas usually outgrow the damage.

In the Pacific Northwest, my biggest problem is pea enation virus, which causes the vines to turn pale and the pods brown and warty. Fortunately, it doesn't appear until the summer really gets warm and the pea harvest is almost over. There are other viruses and wilts that affect peas, but by delaying planting until the soil is warm and

TAKE YOUR PEAS FOR A SWIM

Experts are divided on whether soaking peas before planting is a good idea. My own not-very-scientific tests have shown that it works to improve germination. You can use plain water or a weak, high-quality compost tea. Limit the soaking to no more than 24 hours. After soaking, drain the peas well, then put some garden-pea inoculant—a sooty bacteria powder that helps germination—in a plastic bag. Put the damp peas in the bag and shake it around gently to coat all the peas. Then, plant the seeds immediately.

Inoculant is sold by seed companies, and I regard it as inexpensive insurance. It may not be essential if you've previously grown peas or beans in the same soil, but I use it anyway just to ensure the best chance for pea success.

—Peter Garnham

FOUR WAYS TO STAKE LOW-GROWING PEAS

Like most vines, low-growing peas benefit from some support. If you stick with the shorter varieties, this is an easy job, and you have a number of choices.

LET THE VINES SUPPORT THEMSELVES

If you sow the seeds thickly in a rectangular block, then the vines will grow together into a fairly stable mass. Harvesting involves reaching into the block and picking the pods. I have modified this system by stringing some twine around the entire planting to keep the vines from falling over. A block of peas is worth trying because you can produce a lot of peas in a small space.

CONSTRUCT A TRELLIS

If the trellis is freestanding, seeds can be sown in a row on both sides of the netting. It is better not to plant too thickly; sow the seeds about an inch apart in a single line. Netting or string can also be used against a flat surface, such as a fence or garage. You can plant and harvest from only one side, but you still use very little garden space.

BUILD A BAMBOO STRUCTURE

You can construct a teepee out of bamboo stakes, as you would for runner beans. Keep the legs close together and wrap some string around the whole thing, from bottom to top. Because peas cling by tendrils, they need something narrower than the upright supports to grab on to.

PUT YOUR PRUNINGS TO USE

A common support is known as pea brush: twigs and branches (usually waste you have accumulated from garden maintenance) stuck in the ground in a row. The height of the brush should be equal to or greater than the height listed for the pea variety you're planting. With this method, it is best to make a trench about 6 inches wide and 3 to 4 inches deep for the length of the row. Sow the seeds fairly thickly in this trench, then cover them with soil. This is the easiest time to place the brush, before the seeds germinate. Once again, this makes good use of space. It works best if you can access both sides of the planting for harvest.

Block

Trellis

Pea brush

by planting resistant varieties, you can usually avoid these problems.

By choosing shorter varieties, planting when the soil has warmed up a bit, and harvesting at the right moment, you can enjoy that sweet, fresh taste available only to those who grow their own peas.

Teepee

The time from flower to fruit is short. Once peas start to blossom (above), keep a close eye on the developing pods that follow to make sure you harvest at peak maturity (left).

You may not be able to tell the difference between varieties of sweet corn, aside from white, yellow, and bicolor. Each variety, however, has its own unique characteristics.

GROW YOUR OWN
CORN

Don't be intimidated by corn. Garden writer Jo Ann Gardner reveals that four rows and a little know-how are all you need to grow this summertime treat in your yard.

MY HUSBAND TELLS A STORY ABOUT GROWING UP IN THE 1930S, when his father, on his way home from work, would stop at Mr. Benkendorf's farm stand to buy 'Golden Bantam' corn, and his mother would start boiling water the instant he walked in the door. Why? Because as soon as it was picked, sugar in the corn started turning to starch, and the corn lost its flavor and sweetness—or it used to. That isn't a problem today with the new sweets, a group of hybrids developed over the past 30 years to inhibit the usual rapid sugar-to-starch transfer. You can now enjoy corn that's several days old but still holds its flavor. With so many types of sweet-corn seed varieties available, gardeners can select those that especially suit their needs; older types, like 'Golden Bantam', should be considered, too, for their reliability and for what aficionados regard as their unrivaled, traditional "corny" taste.

Why grow your own corn? Because nothing beats the taste of fresh sweet corn boiled, steamed, or roasted, with butter and salt on the side. It isn't as hard to grow as you might have heard. It requires similar conditions as most vegetables: plenty of sun, sufficient moisture, and enriched soil. And you can grow it in a relatively small space. Sweet corn is best planted in blocks with a minimum of four rows, which maximizes wind pollination. A neat block of tall stalks adds an ornamental dimension to the garden, and when the harvest is over, the corn can be cut down and used for fall decorations. Some gardeners even like the look of corn grown as a garden accent or as a privacy hedge.

GROWING IT RIGHT IS A CINCH

It's no secret that good veggies start with good soil, and corn is no exception. Prepare the ground by spreading rotted manure in fall and working it into the ground the following spring. Poultry manure, high in nitrogen, is especially good for corn, which is a heavy feeder. Compost can be substituted if you don't have access to manure. Scatter a balanced fertilizer (10–10–10) over the area, and rake it in before planting the seed. Because corn roots are shallow and are easily drowned, hill (mound up) the soil if the planting area does not drain well.

When the threat of frost has passed and the soil has warmed up to roughly 60°F, it is time to plant sweet corn. Where soil is late warming, cover the planting area with black plastic to heat it up. Whether the rows are flat or hilled, they should be 2 feet apart, with two or three seeds dropped every 10 inches. Push the seeds about an inch into the soil, and cover them well, tamping them down gently to ensure that they don't get displaced by wind or a hard rain. Once seedlings germinate, thin them to 12 inches apart. In short-season areas, seedlings can be started indoors two weeks before the last frost and planted out when all danger of frost has passed. Add mulch to conserve moisture.

Once the corn plants reach 12 to 18 inches tall, side-dress with a high-nitrogen fertilizer, scratching it into the soil. This gives the plants a boost to grow their leaves and develop their ears. Even if you grow corn under less-than-ideal conditions and don't fertilize, stalks will inevitably bear ears, although they won't be as long or as filled out as they would be when well-fed.

Most stalks bear two or three ears. Begin picking about three weeks after the first silks appear at the top of the ears or when the silks have turned brown. To check for ripeness, pull back the corn husk and squeeze a kernel; if milky juice runs out, the ear is ripe. With experience, you'll be able to judge ripeness at a glance.

You don't need acres of land—just factor in enough space for at least four rows to allow for wind pollination. Space the rows far enough apart for good air circulation to help prevent disease.

HEAD OFF PESTS AND DISEASE

Even when plants are growing well, don't leave them to fend for themselves. Although you may never encounter a serious problem with your crop, keep an eye out for any pests or diseases that could affect performance and yield. The most damaging pests to look for are the larvae of the European corn borer, corn earworm, and fall armyworm. The moths of corn earworms and fall armyworms lay their eggs in corn silks when the silks are green, then the larvae hatch and work their way into the ear. The damage is generally limited to the ear tips and can be cut off at harvest time. Mineral oil poured on the silks (repeated at weekly intervals) can act as a barrier, while neem oil or Pyola can control the larvae when they are small (less than half an inch in length).

PICK THE BEST VARIETY FOR YOU

Maneuvering through the corn section of seed catalogs can be daunting. The main things to watch for are phrases like "widely adaptable"—which assumes a degree of disease resistance—and "days to maturity." Early-season corn is ready to harvest in less than 75 days from sowing, mid-season in 75 to 85 days, and late-season corn in more than 85 days. Grow early-and late-season corn to extend the season, but plant them 30 feet apart, because cross-pollination between different varieties is possible. Isolation is essential with some new sweets.

NAME	DAYS TO MATURITY	DETAILS
'AVALON'	82	A very sweet, sturdy white. Widely adaptable.
'BUTTER AND SUGAR'	73	A tender and sweet variety that is the standard of excellence for bicolor corn.
'CHIPPAWA'	70	A very tender bicolor. Widely adaptable.
'ILLINI XTRA SWEET'	78	A juicy, bright yellow corn. Freezes well.
'KANDY KORN'	89	One of the original sugary enhanced corns, popular for its tender, creamy yellow kernels and distinctive looks: red stalks with corn husks flushed burgundy. Good for freezing or canning. Widely adaptable.
'MONTAUK'	78	A reliable high-sugar bicolor. Widely adaptable.
'POLKA'	59 to 66	A slim-eared bicolor that germinates well in cool soil.
'SENECA HORIZON'	70 to 80	A reliable yellow with good traditional corn flavor.
'SILVER QUEEN'	92	A robust white corn. Sweet and tender yet still retains a traditional taste. In short-season areas, devotees heat up soil in the most favorable site and start plants indoors.
'SPEEDY SWEET'	57 to 64	A vigorous bicolor for short-season areas.
'SWEETIE'	82	A sweet and tender yellow that keeps its sweetness longer than others.
'WHITEOUT'	74	A sturdy-stemmed white with excellent flavor. Widely adaptable.

Neem oil and Pyola also work to control the small larvae of the European corn borer (ECB), though removing the pests by hand works too. ECBs can cause damage all season long, boring into corn stalks and back into the ears as they develop. ECBs lay egg masses on the underside of young leaves. When they are first laid, they are 1/4-inch-long white masses, developing a black head before they hatch. Control is best achieved when the eggs are just hatching, so check corn plants frequently.

ECBs are considered the most serious pest of sweet corn, but during hot weather, aphids may also develop. They can be controlled by using ladybug larvae. Ripe corn also sends signals to local raccoons. Havahart® traps are an effective deterrent.

In addition to these pests, several diseases can also harm your crop: corn smut, corn rust, and northern corn leaf blight. Corn smut appears as large, puffed-out kernels near the tip of the ear, and it releases black spores when broken open. Sweet-corn rust is a late-season disease that produces reddish brown pustules on the bottom of the leaves that release large amounts of spores. Yellowing and necrotic (browning) areas on the leaves could be northern corn leaf blight, and it will substantially weaken the plant. All three of these diseases have no practical control except for the planting of resistant varieties and planting where there is good airflow. Spacing rows 24 to 30 inches apart and planting 1 foot apart in the row will help keep the air moving so that leaves can dry off after experiencing a heavy rain or dew.

Corn plants have shallow roots that won't survive sopping conditions. In places where drainage is not adequate, help keep their heads above water by hilling the soil before planting.

Watch the silks for an easy indicator that your corn is ready to be picked. Silks will begin turning brown when the kernels are mature.

COLORFUL CORN

If the yellow and white color choice of most corn seems too blah for your garden, ornamental corn can jazz things up. Grown for decorative and edible purposes, it comes in a wide range of colors. Plant seeds at least 30 feet from sweet corn and other ornamental varieties. In areas where the season is short, start plants indoors. Harvest ears when their stalks are brown and the kernels are dry to the touch. Complete the drying process indoors or somewhere protected from the elements.

'Hopi Blue' (100 days to maturity) is wind- and drought-tolerant. It dries to an intense blue, and its kernels can be ground into flour.

'Earth Tones' (90 days to maturity), a dent corn, includes colorful kernels of pink, blue, and green.

'Painted Mountain' (85 days to maturity), bred from a Native Indian flour corn for short-season areas, is reported to be impervious to wind, high heat, and cold.

Even with space constraints,
you have plenty of variety
to choose from.

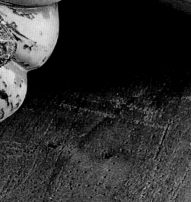

SQUASH IN
TIGHT QUARTERS

Compact bush varieties are the key to growing winter squash in small gardens without sacrificing sweetness. Gardener Glenn Drowns helps you not only choose the right plants but also shares his tips for growing success.

IF YOU HAVE 10 ACRES OF GARDEN, YOU WON'T MIND IF WINTER squash vines sprawl 8 feet in every direction. But if you have a small backyard garden, you can't afford to be so generous. I'm often asked if the space that winter squash takes up is worth the sacrifice. My answer is yes, especially if you grow bush or semi-bush varieties. With these compact plants, the return from even a small patch is high in both quantity and quality.

In addition to being both delicious and prolific, bush squash are also quick to mature—75 to 85 days for most varieties compared with more than 100 days for many vining squash. In areas with a short growing season, bush varieties make a winter-squash crop possible. In areas with a longer growing season, they're an ideal second crop. Late plantings have the additional bonus of avoiding some insect pests. In an 8-foot-long by 4-foot-wide bed, you can plant three hills of bush squash with two or three plants per hill. A planting of this size might yield several dozen squash—not bad from a plot the size of a sheet of plywood.

BUSH SQUASH ARE SHORT ON LEAVES BUT NOT ON FRUIT

A bush squash is one that never produces small side vines. The plants typically take up an area no bigger than 3 feet square. There are also semibush squash, which have dense vines that begin to sprawl but never get very far from the central plant. Semibush plants ultimately take up more space than bush plants, but they tend to yield more fruit, and their sprawling vines can often be tucked back close to the main plant. Given the limited amount of space they cover, both bush and semibush squash produce a lot of fruit.

These compact winter squash, however, are not without drawbacks. Bush squash typically concentrate their fruit set at one time, leaving them susceptible to heavy losses from insect damage. With their single stem and minimal foliage, bush squash are particularly vulnerable to stem-chewing squash vine borers and leaf-feeding squash bugs (see the sidebar on p. 101). Fortunately, semibush squash set fruit in several flushes, giving the plants a chance to replace lost fruit after an insect onslaught. Because foliage helps produce the sugars that feed the fruit, the small amount of foliage on a bush plant can contribute to poorer-tasting flesh. The tendency of some bush varieties to over-produce fruit compounds the problem. But the best of them produce plenty of good-looking, tasty fruit.

This squash is compact enough to fit in a bathtub. Bush varieties, like this 'Emerald Bush Buttercup', grow only 3 to 4 feet wide.

HEALTHY SQUASH PLANTS PRODUCE TASTY FRUIT

I don't hurry to plant winter squash because early plantings have to battle cucumber beetles. My last frost is about April 25, and although bush squash can be planted then, I wait until the third week of May, when the soil has warmed to above 70°F.

Although I often direct-sow my squash, I would recommend setting out transplants in a small garden, where you can't afford heavy losses. Transplants fare better against cucumber beetles, which love emerging seedlings. I set out my transplants when they have fewer than four true leaves; otherwise, the plants will be stunted all season.

Most people plant squash in mounds of soil, known as hills, but I don't bother because my soil is so sandy that the hills disintegrate with the first good rain. I start three seeds per pot, then I plant the root-ball with all three seedlings in one hole—a grouping I refer to as a hill, for lack of a better word. If you prefer to start seedlings one to a pot, you can still plant three seedlings together in one hole; packed close together, they'll help support each other when the wind blows. I space my hills roughly 3 feet apart.

Winter squash are heavy feeders. The ideal soil for growing squash, whether bush or vining, is a smooth, sandy loam with good drainage and lots of organic material. I prefer to feed my squash a mixture of manure and straw from my poultry pens, although at times I use 6-24-24 or 13-13-13 fertilizer. Go easy on the nitrogen, though, or

GROWING COMPACT WINTER SQUASH

- Wait until the soil is above 70°F before planting.
- Plant two or three seedlings per hill, allowing 3 feet between hills.
- Amend the soil with lots of rich organic matter.
- Give plants 1 inch of water per week.
- Harvest before the first frost.

COMPACT SQUASH VARIETIES
THAT MEASURE UP

If you think that small vines mean that compact squash are small on flavor, think again. As long as the plants stay healthy, the fruit will be just as sweet and creamy as regular large-vine varieties. Here are my five favorites for a tiny plot.

'Burpee's Butterbush'   'Sweet Dumpling'   'Golden Acorn'   'Table King'   'Emerald Bush Buttercup'

'BURPEE'S BUTTERBUSH'

'Burpee's Butterbush' is the best of the bush butternuts. It produces small, uniform fruit that usually weigh less than 1 ½ pounds each. 'Burpee's Butterbush', like all butternuts, is highly resistant to squash vine borers because their larvae have trouble chewing their way into the hard stems. This is an enormous advantage in the Midwest and the South. But you must be sure to thin some of the fruit; otherwise, the plants will overproduce, leaving you with squash the size of pickles.

'SWEET DUMPLING'

'Sweet Dumpling' is one of my favorite squash, a relative of acorn squash. This variety has a compact vine most of the season but develops a larger vine toward harvest time. The green-and-white-striped fruit are perfect for a single serving. Their flavor is richer, sweeter, and nuttier than that of other acorn varieties.

'GOLDEN ACORN'

'Golden Acorn' is the best of the bush acorns. It is sometimes called 'Jersey Golden Acorn'.

I find the orange-skinned fruit sweeter and more flavorful than common vining green acorns.

'TABLE KING'

'Table King' is a bush acorn variety whose compact plants are as vigorous as those of most vining varieties. The fruit mature in only 75 days, but they taste much better if allowed to cure on the vine for a few more weeks, until their bottoms turn orange. I thin to five fruit per plant, and if the plant is healthy, all will develop into full-size, full-flavored squash.

'EMERALD BUSH BUTTERCUP'

'Emerald Bush Buttercup' is often billed as a true bush variety, but in my experience, the plants start out as a tidy bush, then send out runners toward the end of the season. The fruit are gray-green, similar to those of most vining buttercups. Their skin is not as thick as that of 'Gold Nugget', so to prevent sunscald and insect damage, harvest the fruit as soon as they mature.

you will end up with foliage that could choke a horse but no fruit.

Give squash 1 inch of water a week but not too much moisture at planting time or the seeds will rot. Mulch looks pretty and keeps squash fruit off the ground in a wet year. But I don't mulch my plants because mulch hides squash bugs and its added moisture tends to induce rot in the plants. The bottom line is that a healthy squash plant produces the best fruit. This is because a stressed plant uses sugars to keep going rather than to feed its fruit.

HAUL IN A FULL-SIZE HARVEST

Bush winter squash should be harvested before the first frost because squash subjected to frost don't keep well. To determine whether a winter squash is ready to harvest, poke the skin with your fingernail. If your nail leaves a mark, the squash is still immature (see the photo at right). I never rush to pick a squash. Even if it looks ripe and passes the fingernail hardness test, I wait a week or two before harvesting it. Squash allowed to mature fully on the vine keep longer in storage.

After being picked, winter squash improve in flavor if allowed to cure for a week or two. Harvested fruit should be kept outside in a warm and sunny place for a few days, then stored in a dry indoor environment with a temperature of around 55°F. The fruit from most compact winter-squash plants keep for three to nine months—butternuts the longest, acorns the shortest—so you can enjoy home-grown produce in the dreary days of winter.

Use your fingers to determine ripeness. If your fingernail doesn't leave an imprint, the squash is ready to pick.

GROW THEM UP INSTEAD OF OUT

When you have a small amount of space, growing pumpkins is usually out of the question. But that doesn't have to be the case. Pumpkins are vines that you can train to grow vertically. In my urban garden, I use a chain-link fence for support. Throughout the growing season, I train the vines to grow up and through the fence. The tendrils also help, by wrapping around the wire fence and supporting the plant as it grows. The best types of pumpkins to grow vertically are smaller varieties, like 'Jack Be Little', a tiny, flat, 8-ounce pumpkin, or 'New England Pie', a 4- to 5-pound sweet pumpkin perfect for pies.

—Patti Moreno

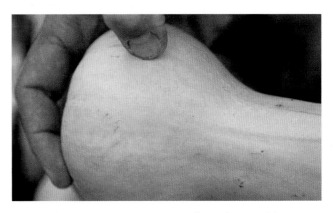

SQUASH PLANT FOES

I grow acres of squash and melons, so I've seen all kinds of squash pests. The cucumber beetle, the squash vine borer, and the squash bug, however, are the ones that cause the most damage. But they are all easy to control, especially in a small squash patch.

Squash vine borer

CUCUMBER BEETLE

Cucumber beetles, which can be striped or spotted, arrive when temperatures are between 75°F and 85°F. A chewing insect that relishes germinating seeds and squash blossoms, the cucumber beetle can wipe out young winter-squash seedlings in a matter of hours. With quick-growing bush squash in particular, the way I deal with cucumber beetles is simply to avoid them by planting a late crop. I sometimes plant bush varieties as late as July 4.

SQUASH VINE BORER

The squash vine borer is the most destructive squash pest, especially of bush-squash varieties, and also the hardest to control. Beginning in mid-June, the clear-winged adult moths fly from plant to plant, laying eggs at their base. When the eggs hatch, the larvae burrow into the stem and proceed to grow into fat, 1-inch-long white grubs, which feed on the stem tissue, choking off food to the plant. If squash vine borers destroy the central stem of a vining squash, side stems that have rooted can take over. But if they destroy the only stem of a bush squash,

the plant is doomed. The first indication of squash vine borers is a plant that wilts at mid-day. When you see a watered and otherwise healthy plant wilt, check its base for a sawdust-like residue. If you see any, split open the stem with a knife and remove the larvae, then cover the stem with moist soil. The plant will usually recover.

SQUASH BUG

Another pest waiting for tasty young seedlings is the squash bug. Juice-sucking squash bugs overwinter in garden refuse and woodpiles, and they arrive with the emergence of the first squash plant. A heavy concentration of squash bugs on the precious few leaves of a bush-squash plant often spells disaster. I control squash bugs with a good garden cleanup after the harvest. In midwinter, I spot-check the garden edges for adult squash bugs, which are slow moving and easy to catch and squish. A late squash planting will avoid the first few generations of squash bugs and possibly prevent an exponential population buildup. Handpicking these pests is easy and effective.

DECORATIVE GARDENS

Garden with every season in mind. Asian-inspired hardscaping combined with foliage-focused plantings keeps this space interesting year-round.

✓ **DESIGN IDEAS**
✓ **HARDSCAPE**
✓ **CONTAINER GARDEN**

DESIGNING
SMALL-SPACE GARDENS

Landscape designer Rebecca Sams used texture and foliage to transform a tiny, paved backyard into a tranquil, Japanese-inspired retreat. By adding a hardscape layer to a concrete patio, she brought homeowners' Ted and Nancy Dobson's vision to life.

ALL TED AND NANCY DOBSON WANTED WAS A SIMPLE CONTAINER garden. But when my partner and I first met with them, we discovered that the Dobsons' backyard looked more like the bottom of a swimming pool than a patio. It was a little space, with house and garage walls on one side, a shoulder-high retaining wall on the other, and a river of concrete in between. The tight dimensions made the yard feel closed in, and we couldn't remove the paving due to drainage issues. The Dobsons hoped, however, that adding several pretty planters would at least soften the look.

Although it would have been simple enough to install a container garden, we knew that none of us would be ecstatic about the results. This property presented some imposing challenges, which were beyond the help of planters. We solved almost every problem at once, however, by building an elevated garden above the pavement and applying a few design techniques that would improve almost any small space.

DESIGN USING FOLIAGE AND BOLD DETAILS

Ted and Nancy chose a visually quiet palette of greens, silvers, and burgundies, and they selected foliage-centric plants, which give the garden structure year-round. As this garden would be their only outdoor living space, it was vital to select plants that look as striking in June as they do in October. The plantings change subtly throughout the year but include almost no seasonal color from flowers, which would have left noticeable holes when they were out of bloom.

The focus on lush foliage reflects the Dobsons' desire for a tranquil space. Pops of bright, saturated color, which a large garden could easily absorb, would have overwhelmed this little backyard. Like much of the garden, the plantings are inspired by the work of Japanese garden designers who, through the centuries, have understood that a mostly neutral color palette with contrasting textures and forms can make a small garden engaging and soothing.

People too often clutter small gardens with small objects. For this space, however, we strategically placed large containers to create a bold, clean look. Three tall, conical, Vietnamese planters (#1, site plan, p. 108) between the deck and retaining wall provide a quiet focal point, visible from multiple angles in the garden. The containers' size and location give them a strong presence, while their simple, unadorned shapes and solid colors allow them to coordinate effortlessly with other elements.

BEFORE

The mini concrete-covered space was transformed into an oasis.

AFTER

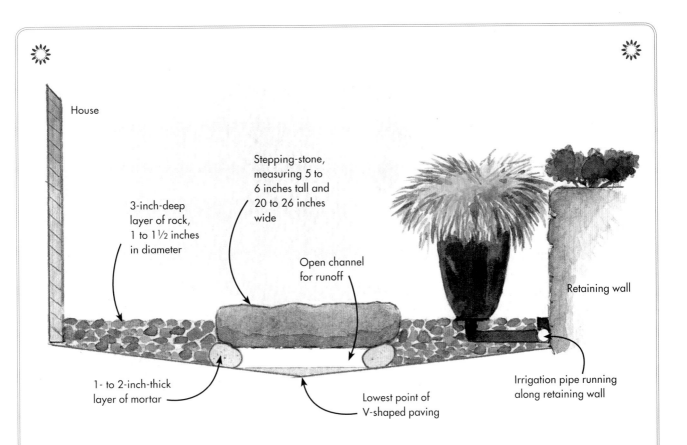

House

Stepping-stone, measuring 5 to 6 inches tall and 20 to 26 inches wide

3-inch-deep layer of rock, 1 to 1½ inches in diameter

Open channel for runoff

Retaining wall

1- to 2-inch-thick layer of mortar

Lowest point of V-shaped paving

Irrigation pipe running along retaining wall

DISGUISING THE CONCRETE WITHOUT HINDERING DRAINAGE

The Dobsons' original paved backyard was an unusual starting point, to say the least. Although removing the concrete was tempting, the drainage path created by the slightly V-shaped surface was necessary to keep water away from the house. So building over the concrete was our best option.

There is no visual sign today of the concrete subsurface, but the original drainage system continues to work perfectly. Small, round river rock covers the pavement and the irrigation piping while still allowing rainwater to run to the drains. This local river rock is both aesthetically beautiful and practical. Due to the rounded shape of the stones, water runs through them quickly, and because the stones are without a powdery surface, they don't clog the drains

with fine particles. This gravel also has a bold texture, which makes it stand out, and a light, neutral color, which nicely contrasts with the garden's other hardscape elements. Thick basalt stepping-stones, spaced 2 to 3 inches apart and mortared beneath for stability, provide a solid surface for walking or even rolling a wheelbarrow. We borrowed this idea from Japanese gardens, which often have narrow, noncontinuous paths that make visitors move slowly and deliberately through a space, looking down at the path to place their steps carefully and up again to discover new views of the garden. This narrowing of focus enhances the experience of traveling through the Dobsons' passageway.

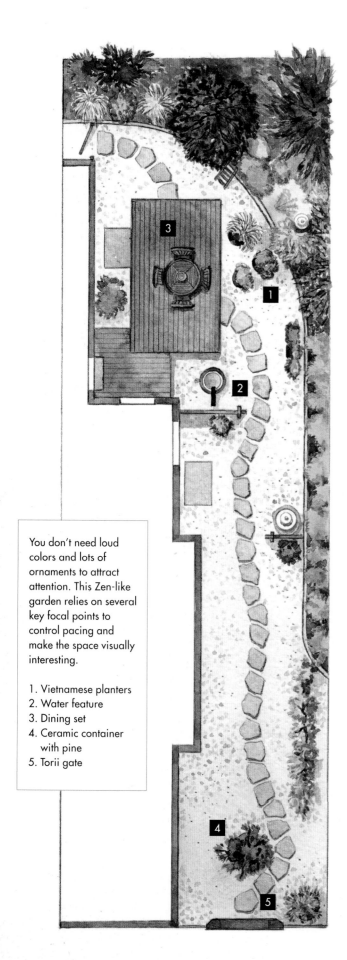

You don't need loud colors and lots of ornaments to attract attention. This Zen-like garden relies on several key focal points to control pacing and make the space visually interesting.

1. Vietnamese planters
2. Water feature
3. Dining set
4. Ceramic container with pine
5. Torii gate

The Dobsons further improved the space by replacing a grouping of small pots near the deck with a stately water feature (#2). Bringing such a large focal point into a tight space concerned them at first, but the feature fell into place perfectly. It is broad enough to stand alone and tall enough to complement the 6-foot-tall bamboo screen directly behind it. When accessorizing a small space, pick containers, water features, and other ornaments that are too substantial to ignore and yet not so big that they feel shoehorned into place.

Limited space doesn't mean you must settle for a cramped seating area. When it comes to spaces for entertaining, function is foremost. After all, if it doesn't work well, you won't use it. The Dobsons' ample hardscape is both serene and practical. While many small spaces have only a tiny café table with a pair of chairs, this ipe deck comfortably seats four (#3). The opposite problem of oversizing, of course, was a risk, which is why we left so much breathing room around the ipe deck (see the bottom photo on the facing page). At an absolute minimum, leave space for people to easily walk by empty furniture, and make sure that guests can scoot their chairs out without falling over an edge. Just a couple of feet is often enough buffer to make a seating area inviting.

ENCLOSE THE SPACE TO BLOCK VISUAL DISTRACTIONS

People naturally look right past small spaces, unless something obstructs or focuses their view. Defining boundaries with fences, gates, screens, or focal points keeps the viewer's attention within a small area. Selecting the right borders can enhance a garden as much as a well-planned seating area or plant palette.

In the Dobsons' garden, a pair of bamboo screens divides two small garden rooms with distinct purposes: a seating area and a passageway. The screens enclose each garden, holding attention inside that space. In the entertaining area, the screens provide the final walls of the room, making it feel intimate while providing a subtle, textural backdrop for Asian-inspired accent pieces. From within the passageway, the bamboo backdrop keeps visitors' attention on their journey along the stepping-stone path (see the bottom photo on p. 106). By staggering the screens, we created a visual barrier from some perspectives and a framed view from others. When visitors walk toward the screens on the stepping-stone path, new parts of the garden are gradually but continually revealed, drawing visitors into the following space.

At the opposite end of the passageway garden, stepping-stones bend around a sculptural pine in a large ceramic container (#4). Although this feature is far from a solid barrier, it provides a focal point and a visual stop at the end of the path. Without it, attention would just follow the stone path through the torii gate (#5) and out of the garden. The feature and gate, instead, work together to make a striking backdrop for a peaceful little space (see the photo at right).

RIGHT Give visitors reasons to slow down. It's hard to walk past this Japanese-inspired gate without pausing to take a closer look.

BELOW Consider the view at eye level. This ipe deck floats above the river rock, just high enough so that those seated at the table look directly at the plantings, not at the retaining wall.

THERE'S BIG POTENTIAL IN
SMALL SPACES

A small city lot can still be a dream garden. Just follow gardener Jennie Hammill's advice to create your own garden oasis.

IT'S BEEN SAID THAT YOU CAN TELL A LOT ABOUT PEOPLE BY their gardens. I think mine says that my life is full and varied. As a certified plantaholic, I yearn for 2 acres with large, sweeping beds and borders and some vegetable and cutting gardens. But having only a small city lot (40 feet wide by 100 feet long) as my canvas, I've had to come up with some creative ways to get the most out of my space. I'm not really greedy—my only wish is to have one of everything.

My initial step was to look at every imaginable part of my property as a potential spot for a garden. I then had to figure out a way to deal with some conditional drawbacks that often plague small spaces, like heavy root competition. And finally, I decided not to give up on outdoor entertaining areas—just to reconfigure them. Using a few key strategies allowed me to create the garden of my dreams, albeit on a smaller scale.

Make your big dreams a reality—even in a small space. Lush plantings, numerous containers, a patio, and even a few seating areas were all squeezed into this tiny city lot.

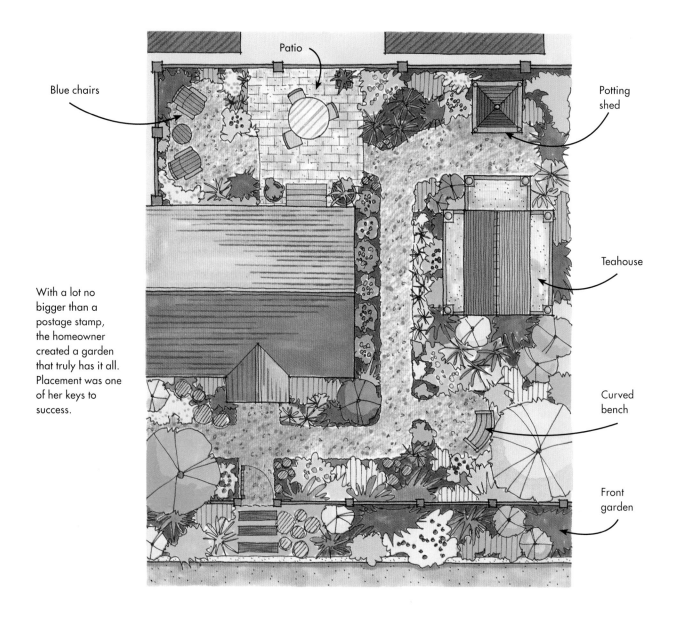

Blue chairs

Patio

Potting shed

Teahouse

With a lot no bigger than a postage stamp, the homeowner created a garden that truly has it all. Placement was one of her keys to success.

Curved bench

Front garden

LEAVE NO SPOT UNPLANTED

Given my limitations, something had to go, and the easiest thing for me to give up was lawn. I admire lawns in larger spaces for framing borders and beds or for playing croquet, but for me, it just wasn't practical. Being an avid gardener with a limited amount of land, I plant every available inch of space—even spots that most gardeners would consider completely inhospitable. But my hope is to be surrounded and welcomed by plants from the curb, down the side of the house, and all the way to the back garden.

At the front of my house is a rocky hill that serves as a retaining wall of sorts. Although not the ideal area for a garden, I didn't want to give up this potential planting

A front entry can be more than just functional. When space is at a premium, even a rocky, curbside retaining wall should be seen as a golden gardening opportunity.

LEFT Put your pots on a pedestal. Elevate containers to draw the eye down a path and to add a focal point in an otherwise unfocused area.

BELOW Not every container needs to be a pot. The lush plantings along the side of the house could be suffocating, but delightful containers, such as this antique birdcage, add interest and structure to the scene.

parcel. My goal was grand: to make the space abundant and welcoming, with something always in bloom; to give a nod to its neighboring environment; and to offer something a little different and special. Even though it wasn't a conventional spot to put a garden, it's the only part of my property that gets more than six hours of sunlight, so I filled the curbside planting with small shrubs that have year-round interest and flowers in continual bloom. I then moved on to plant every other nook and cranny of the property.

Planting every available inch can start to make your garden feel unruly if you're not careful. But when I first began gardening, I heard a phrase that really struck me. It was something like "Bare soil expresses the poverty of the soul." Heaven forbid. In my desire to have a lush, filled-in, and mature look, my garden soon became too busy and untamed. I had an underlying fear that if I turned my back for a few weeks, the house would be eaten up by the garden and disappear. I think I will spend all my life trying to find a happy balance between full and lush and way too much, but I continue to fill every spot with plants, then go back to edit and space them to achieve a better effect.

GET MORE STRUCTURE AND DEPTH BY USING CONTAINERS

With so many plants, I needed to add definition to the chaos. One way I did this was to place pots right into the beds. Containers add a structural element to the plantings and break things up visually. They also provide a splash of color. Designers often tell you to stick to just one pot color in a small space, but this is something I have failed at miserably. (I can be disciplined in many areas of life but not in pot selection.) I have tried, though, to group my containers somewhat by color or in close proximity to a piece of architecture with a similar hue. My red pots, for example, echo the color of some nearby French doors. Pots also help soften the boundaries of my property.

By placing the containers a bit forward, rather than tucked up against the back fence or the sides of the house, I am able to add depth—making the walls seem farther away. This helps me feel like the borders of my lot are disappearing. As a bonus, these containers can also be used to define sight lines, such as placing a pot on a stand at the end of a path—similar to English gardens that use statues on their grand estates but on a scale that works for me.

Containers give me better control over soil and water issues too. Like many small spaces that are packed with plants, my beds have a lot of root competition. My soil is sandy, and although I faithfully amend the soil each year, some things grow far better for me in containers. Hostas (*Hosta* spp. and cvs., USDA Hardiness Zones 3–9), for instance, will shrink down in size and gradually wither away if left in the ground. Even hydrangeas (*Hydrangea* spp. and cvs., Zones 4–9), which are supposedly drought tolerant once established, look pathetic in the ground. Some rhododendrons (*Rhododendron* spp. and cvs., Zones 5–9) became so eaten by root weevils—because they were stressed by dry soil—that even they are in large pots now. Containers placed under trees are a godsend: There is no root and water competition, and the potted plants help fill that vertical void between the soil and tree canopy.

Plus, pots allow me to move things around. When plants enter my garden, it's understood that they will have to play many rounds of musical chairs. Just because my space is tight doesn't mean I can't shake things up every now and then.

LEFT Decorative pots and hanging baskets allow you to add flowers but not roots to already crowded beds.

BELOW Don't abandon your wish list—just scale it down. Entertaining areas and even a potting shed can be incorporated on your tiny property as long as you reduce their size.

DOWNSIZE YOUR SEATING AREAS, BUT DON'T ELIMINATE THEM

Although my lot is packed with plants, I didn't give up spots to sit back and enjoy. I strategically placed seating to maximize the longest sight lines and to define outdoor rooms. I also paid attention to what was behind a specific area. In the backyard, for example, blue chairs occupy the farthest corner of the property. With the fence at your back, the views of neighboring houses are eliminated, giving a sense of privacy in the city, while the fence provides a feeling of security. The path to the chairs offers a sense of journey and destination. Best of all, by viewing the garden on a diagonal, the space looks bigger.

In the entry courtyard, I strategically placed a semi-round bench at an angle. The curve of the bench helps enclose and define the small outdoor room and encourages people to move around the corner to the side garden, while the fence and small ornamental cherry tree behind it act like enveloping arms. The view from the bench down the long side of the house is the longest my garden can offer, so it was important to make sure that there was a spot to pause and take in this modest expanse.

I even built a 10-foot-wide by 14-foot-long garden house (that I call the "teahouse") at the back corner of the property. It might seem crazy given my space limitations, but I wanted a special place to sit and take in the surrounding beauty. Again, placement was key. From the inside of the teahouse, the garden looks expansive. And from the outside, the reflective qualities of the glass windows and doors not only bounce more light around the garden but also add a dimension of depth. When the light is right, you can see behind, into, and beyond the enclosure, which creates a magical sense of space. I was worried that adding a larger structure to the property might make my garden seem even smaller, but I found the opposite to be true.

With a little creativity and an unwillingness to give up my desire for a lush and varied garden, I was able to use my space limitations to my advantage. Although, if you offered me just a few more feet, I'm sure I could find a few plants to fill it.

ABOVE There should always be a place to sit and enjoy. A large outbuilding, such as this teahouse, usually gets nixed from a small-space design plan, but if it is placed in a spot that maximizes sight lines, it doesn't seem out of place.

LEFT Provide a destination. A narrow passageway that is crammed full of plants would seem chaotic if there weren't a comfortable chair to focus on during the journey.

A sunken seating area adds intimacy, while the plants and decorative objects that dress up the surroundings make it more comfortable.

A TOWNHOUSE
GARDEN ROOM

Homeowner Becca Robinson knew her new home's small yard needed a radical overhaul as soon as she bought it. So she added privacy and plants to make this outdoor room the perfect garden for a party. Former Fine Gardening *assistant editor Daryl Beyers reveals the plan she followed to transform her space.*

NESTLED ALONG A QUIET STREET IN THE CHERRY CREEK neighborhood of Denver, Colorado, is a gem of a garden that epitomizes the casual comfort of outdoor living. Becca Robinson's garden is an outdoor room approximately 30 feet wide by 70 feet long. Set in alongside her modest house, this walled oasis plays host to spontaneous gatherings of neighbors and friends who come and go, visiting, chatting, and laughing together each Friday evening. They call it "Doing Friday," and each week is a testament to the usefulness of this intimate space.

Becca moved into her late-19th-century adobe-style townhouse in 2004. At the time, the garden consisted of an ugly stone patio off a concrete stoop leading from the living-room door. Becca took one look at that dysfunctional space and decided to seize its potential as an extension of the house. She wanted a place where she could sip her morning tea, enjoy dinner with friends, and relax with a good book at the end of the day.

ADDING WALLS

The house forms one wall of the garden room, and a back wall is created by a neighboring townhouse, but two additional lengths of wall were needed to properly enclose the space. Becca negotiated with her neighbors to build the new walls 8 feet high, rather than the 6-foot height that the code allowed, to ensure the privacy she wanted in her urban environment. The first new wall continues along the property line. In the other new wall, which faces the street, Becca put an entry gate with open bar work, through which glimpses of bright blooms or the sound of friendly laughter from within attract passersby and welcome visitors to the party.

WITHIN THE WALLS

Exiting the living room down a set of wide steps, visitors enter a dining area backed by an elegant outdoor fireplace and sheltered by a well-crafted pergola. The fireplace breaks up an expanse of garden wall and also creates an

The change in grade also allows for controlled drainage of the entire garden. Water naturally collects in the lower spot and is handled by a drainage system installed during construction.

A consistent use of brick throughout the garden visually unites these spaces, making partygoers feel connected to the festivities no matter what part of the garden they find themselves in. A brick path further ties the garden together by running from the city sidewalk through the entry gate, past a barbecue and the sunken sitting area to the dining room, and then around a perennial border to the rear of the house. By using the same brick throughout, the patio and paths become an integrated whole that reinforces the garden's comfortable union of indoors and outdoors.

PLANTS SET THE STYLE

The borders dress up the garden walls and building façades with a simple palette of plants. When it comes to small trees and shrubs, Becca has chosen to live with much of what was there when she arrived: a cottonless cottonwood (*Populus deltoides* 'Siouxland', USDA Hardiness Zones 3–9), ivy (*Hedera* spp. and cvs., Zones 5–11) on the walls, and an old lilac (*Syringa vulgaris* cv., Zones 4–8). She has decided to keep them until she finds an opportunity to replace them. Becca never removes a plant until she has a replacement waiting in the wings. "Any plant is better than a hole," she says.

With the perennials, however, plant combinations come and go as she "pops 'em in, then moves 'em around." Akin to the comings and goings of Friday's garden guests, any plant may unexpectedly appear in the borders. Oftentimes, after a month or two, a plant will return to its original spot. It's a game she enjoys.

Container plantings are an important part of the spontaneous, casual atmosphere of this garden. They add foliage and flowers to the patio and soften the hard corners of the brick steps and walkways. All the pots are on a drip-irrigation system and are often used in the same location in consecutive seasons, although the herbaceous plantings change from year to year. Becca says they are not different on purpose; she simply can never remember what they were the previous year. Openness to change and an outgoing attitude keep this small urban garden fresh and vibrant, continuing the party year after year.

ABOVE Containers add depth and variety that break up the expanses of brick, while the vintage shutters ease the brightness of the white-stuccoed wall.

LEFT Open-air entertaining is more inviting with the right amenities, like this handsome pergola over the dining table and a nearby conversation pit.

instant focal point that draws guests to the large dining table. The pergola lets in light, but a shade pulled over its top lessens the bright Colorado sun, making it more comfortable to sit there in the daytime. More important, the pergola creates a ceiling for the outdoor dining room, suggesting the comfort of having a roof over one's head.

Spaces are also defined by changes in elevation. A seating area off the dining space lies 2 feet below the main grade, signaling the change to a setting where dinner guests can relax after their meal (see the photo on p. 116).

MAKE A SMALL SPACE
FEEL BIGGER

Backyards often back up to neighbor's fences and other unsightly, mismatched backgrounds. Garden designer Jeffrey Bale was faced with this challenge in Tim O'Hearn's tight backyard. But armed with a design plan that created distinct spaces—and camouflaged the disparate views—he was able to create the paradise that Tim asked for.

AS A DESIGNER AND BUILDER OF GARDENS, I'M OFTEN challenged to transform a forlorn yard into a personal Eden. When I first met with my client Tim O'Hearn in his backyard in Portland, Oregon, this proved to be the case once again. He envisioned a secluded paradise with a place for enjoying a morning cup of coffee, a space for dining and entertaining, and a hot tub to soak away stress. He also wanted lush plantings, a fishpond,

BEFORE

This small yard (left) lacked a sense of seclusion. A design with a two-level terrace and lush plantings (far left) makes it feel like a private paradise.

BEFORE

The house and backyard consisted of a mishmash of design styles and elements that added up to the feeling that the space was not inviting.

A Unattractive, mismatched fencing

B No greenery to screen out upper floors of neighboring houses

C Unappealing patio spaces, covered by aluminum awnings

D A lumpy, sloping lawn, with no specific spaces for entertaining and relaxing

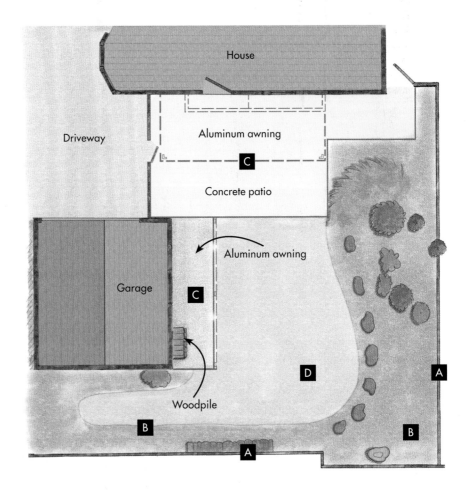

AFTER

To make the site more inviting and usable, the space was divided into a series of interconnected rooms.

A Fences are covered with reed panels

B Privacy is created with tall bamboo and other plantings along the perimeter

C An arbor adds feeling of privacy to lower terrace

D The upper terrace, ringed by low stone walls, is home to a dining area, a claw-foot tub, and a water garden

SITE: 30 feet wide by 40 feet long

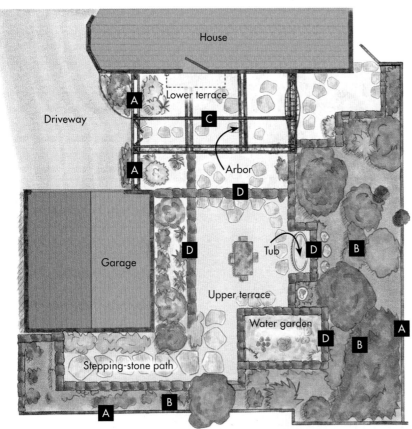

a shaded arbor for growing vines, and a place to grow vegetables—all in an area about 30 feet wide by 40 feet long. The small backyard had a host of problems with which I had to contend. It was bounded by a garage and three different styles of neighboring fences (see the photo on p. 121). Neighboring houses also had views of the yard. A cracked-concrete patio against the back of the house was covered with the kind of aluminum awning typically seen attached to trailer homes (see the photo at right), and a similar awning hung along one side of the garage. The lawn was a lumpy slope edged with weed-filled beds of scraggly azaleas and rhododendrons. Despite these eyesores and challenges, I assured Tim that we could create a lush and private garden in which he would feel completely at home.

BEFORE

ABOVE An aluminum awning and a concrete patio next to the house were removed to make way for an intimate terrace.

LEFT Low stone walls, which surround the raised beds and water garden, double as seating. Gold-leaved plants serve as bright accents against the darker stone.

A SOLID PLAN ADDRESSES PROBLEMS

To begin the problem-solving process, I measured the site and drew up a base plan. Using copies of the plan, I developed several loose schematic designs to address the site's problems and to create a layout that would meet Tim's wish list.

To gain privacy from the neighbors, there needed to be tall screens of plantings in certain areas. The space where the driveway connected to the garden also required screening and a gate.

To unify the appearance of the existing fences, I suggested covering them with a material made of Chinese reeds. These durable, strawlike reeds are woven with wire into 20-foot-long rolls, which are easy to cut and staple onto wood fences.

One way to deal with a slope is to terrace it to create usable, flat space. Since the grade in this yard was not steep, I decided to divide the space into two levels and to make 18-inch-high walls, which could double as places for sitting and for setting objects (see the bottom photo on p. 123). I mortared the walls for solidity, using broken concrete rubble from the patio demolition to build up the back sides. In the center of the upper terrace, I used pea gravel spread over landscape fabric to economize on paving stones and to minimize rainwater runoff. I made a step between the two patio levels to reduce both the amount of excavation required and the impact on tree roots (see the photo above).

For the walls and terraces, Tim and I selected a local stone with rich brown tones. The house had been painted a dull gray that did not enhance the architecture or the garden, so we decided to repaint the house a rich chocolate brown with burgundy trim, which looks attractive with the stone. The dark colors actually make the house recede visually so that its scale feels less dominating. I designed a high arbor to connect to the back of the house and to add to the feeling of privacy on the lower terrace. This arbor brings the towering façade of the house into scale with the garden and creates a pleasing transitional area. I also installed a gated entry where the driveway meets the lower terrace (see the photo below).

A SMALL SPACE CATERS TO SEVERAL ACTIVITIES

The goal in arranging the space was to make room for different living activities by creating interconnected areas. The upper level is designated as a space for dining and entertaining. In addition to adding structure to the space, the low stone walls serve as seating without taking up extra space. The square angles of the walls reinforce the sense that the garden is an extension of the house, albeit without a roof.

FACING PAGE A slightly higher upper terrace addresses the yard's slope while creating a space that is distinct from a lower terrace near the house.

RIGHT A reed-covered entry gate leads from the driveway to the lower terrace.

Plantings disguise the reed-covered perimeter fencing and soften the hard edges of the stone walls next to the stepping-stone path.

A claw-foot, plumbed bathtub is nestled within a niche of raised-bed planters.

To create a cozy space for enjoying morning coffee, we placed a small table and two chairs under the arbor on the lower terrace next to the house. I made the arbor 9 feet tall to keep that space open and airy. We chose a seedless table grape (*Vitis labrusca* 'Suffolk Red', USDA Hardiness Zones 5–8) to grow up the posts of the arbor; its fruit matches the house's new trim color. The sturdy 6×6 cedar posts also provided the perfect place to hang a hammock. To address Tim's desire for a water feature, I built a rectangular 6-foot by 10-foot fishpond into two intersecting walls at the back of the garden. A simple fountain pro-

vides the sound of running water. From there, the wall continues as a raised bed in a thin strip of land behind the garage (see the photo on the facing page). Because this backyard garden is so functional and inviting, it's no surprise that it gets used on a daily basis. It's the perfect place to read the morning paper, share meals, or just relax. Tim also loves to take a hot bath in the claw-foot tub, enjoying the scent of jasmine and the sounds of trickling water and bamboo leaves rustling in the breeze. It sounds like Eden to me.

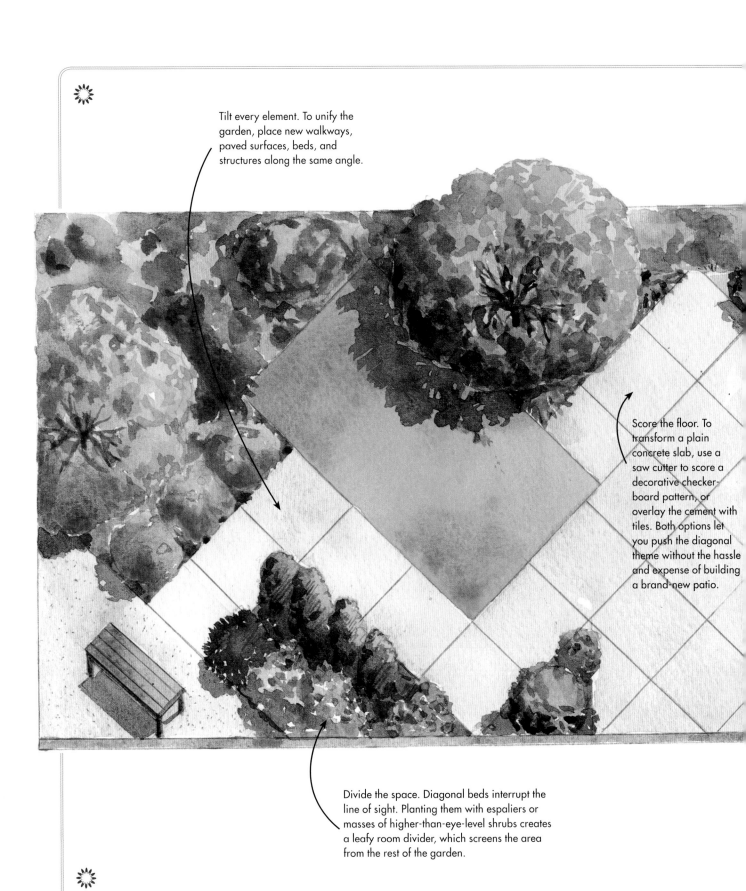

Tilt every element. To unify the garden, place new walkways, paved surfaces, beds, and structures along the same angle.

Score the floor. To transform a plain concrete slab, use a saw cutter to score a decorative checker-board pattern, or overlay the cement with tiles. Both options let you push the diagonal theme without the hassle and expense of building a brand-new patio.

Divide the space. Diagonal beds interrupt the line of sight. Planting them with espaliers or masses of higher-than-eye-level shrubs creates a leafy room divider, which screens the area from the rest of the garden.

Maximize deep corners. You can soften corners with a vine-covered trellis (set on the diagonal, of course), layered plantings, or an eye-catching focal point, such as a fountain or sculpture.

Rearrange the furniture. Wake things up by laying a striped all-weather rug on a 45-degree angle, then align the table and chairs along the same axis.

Punch it up with plants. Emphasize the skewed layout by outlining the seating area with planted containers, preferably square pots and rectangular troughs.

LANDSCAPE ARCHITECT
BILLY GOODNICK'S

ADVICE FOR DESIGNING ON THE DIAGONAL

You don't have to be Pythagoras to see the value of creating a diagonal sight line through a garden. Kicking paths, patios, and focal points off-kilter is an easy way to enliven a boxy backyard and create the illusion of more space.

Whereas traditional layouts reveal everything at first glance, gardens designed on an angle have more intrigue. Because the hypotenuse is the longest distance between opposite corners, drawing attention to it makes a small garden seem longer. This lengthening effect gets more dramatic as the angle gets more acute. And here's another bonus: Designing along a diagonal results in extra-deep corner beds, which means you'll have even more room for plants.

So whether you're starting with a blank slate or wanting to give your garden a fresh look, don't be timid about skewing around inside the box. There are a number of creative ways to slant your space.

The purple house is only one indication that something interesting is happening in this otherwise unassuming lot. What was once all driveway is now several unique garden rooms.

PINT-SIZE
GARDEN SPACES

Even a small garden area can host a variety of entertaining spaces. Follow cookbook author Lucinda Hutson's recipe for success to create multiple mini garden rooms that give guests plenty to admire while making the space seem larger.

I LOVE COOKING AND ENTERTAINING, SO I KNOW HOW A SIMPLE meal can become a grand feast by stretching it out one tasty course at a time. I have taken a similar approach with my small property, dividing it into individual portions to make it appear larger than it is. Each area has its own flavor and personality and is filled with elements of surprise and delight. I have garnished my gardens with color, texture, and flair, as one would adorn a festive platter of food.

My lot is only 50 feet wide and 135 feet long. Within this small space I have created appealing yet functional gardens that complement the Tex-Mex tradition of my home and showcase the artistry of my friends. My guests embark on an enchanted journey through a succession of outdoor rooms, greeted by a fiesta of fresh herbs, flowers, folk art, and whimsy, never suspecting that my property is as small as it is. Anyone who wants to create a garden that seems bigger than its size can follow my recipe.

It takes visitors a while to absorb the different areas and their unique elements. By experiencing my garden in these small servings, both my visitors and I feel relaxed and satisfied, something anyone who loves to entertain strives for.

CREATE A SENSE OF DIVISION

I considered my driveway to be wasted space, so I converted it into a garden. I had a stonemason build a 6-foot-high wall aligned with the front of the house and attached to an ornate entry gate. The wall's dry-stacked, cut limestone—a native Texas element—adds rustic appeal and a sturdy sense of privacy. I assembled an 8-foot-square glass greenhouse in the middle of the driveway to transform the space on either side into distinct rooms. The front area became a fishpond (see the top photo at left), the back, a Mexican courtyard (see the center photo at left). In the fishpond area, I created a "living wall" by lining the limestone wall with large, native river rocks that are irregularly shaped and full of holes. The spaces provide perfect niches for planting. I also encrusted the stones with small seashells, mosaics, and tiles.

The purple walls of the garage-turned-toolshed and the house flank the Mexican courtyard. The walls aren't imposing because they are outdoor art galleries displaying colorful children's chairs and other folk-art treasures from my south-of-the-border travels. The greenhouse, adorned with cedar trellises and vines (see the bottom photo at left), serves as another border of this courtyard. Peering through the windows, I can catch a glimpse of the fishpond.

A fence of unpeeled, split-cedar posts adds privacy and maintains the Tex-Mex theme. Staggered in height from 5 feet to 8 feet, the posts make a verdant backdrop when draped with vines. By making the numerous walls of my

TOP The area between the greenhouse and the limestone wall became the fishpond.

CENTER Changes in elevation create interest. Raising the kitchen garden forms a distinct area within the Mexican courtyard.

BOTTOM What was once a driveway is now a series of garden rooms. Placing the greenhouse in the middle of what was the driveway created two rooms on either side.

Lowering the back patio creates a distinct area just as well as raising it would have.

Changing paving materials and patterns can signal transitions to distinct areas such as the back patio.

garden visually appealing, softening them with natural materials, and ensuring that other areas are visible from any room, I've divided my space without adding a sense of confinement.

RAISE SOME AREAS, LOWER OTHERS

Visitors often have to step up or down as they move through my small property. These steps delineate different areas, which creates a sense of spaciousness. In the Mexican courtyard, I wanted my 10-foot-square kitchen garden, brimming with colors, textures, and aromas, to be the center of attention, like a stunning floral ar-

rangement. I raised it $2^1/_2$ feet, using the same dry-stack limestone as in the front wall. The repetition of materials provides continuity from space to space. The ledge created in this area offers extra seating, while the raised floor promotes the good drainage necessary for growing healthy herbs and vegetables.

The back patio drops 2 feet, but the effect is the same as with the raised areas. The changes in elevation signal transitions between spaces and create the sense that each room is distinct. Visitors don't get the feeling that the property is one big, partitioned space but rather a garden of unique spaces full of surprises.

MYSTERY MAKES
A SMALL SPACE FEEL BIGGER

Make your small backyard feel expansive without losing its intimate feel. Landscape designer and contractor Keith Davitt did just that by dividing the space, terracing the land, and using curves and diagonals to slowly reveal the many aspects of his garden.

FOR ME, THE INTENT OF LANDSCAPE DESIGN IS TO CREATE an environment that's both wonderful to see and delightful to experience. This environment is more easily realized where space is plentiful and options are endless. In urban sites, however, space is limited. So how, then, do you create the fun of discovery, the peace of solitude, and the delight of visual intrigue, and divest these little urban yards of that sense of confinement so many of them seem to convey? After several years of finding solutions that satisfied my clients and me, I am convinced that there is no site—no matter how small—that cannot be effectively transformed. Chances are a tiny plot awaits only the application of a few of these principles before it, too, becomes a garden that gives lasting pleasure.

Nestled at the back of the garden is a seating area and a fishpond, which serves as the focal point for visitors wandering to the end of the garden path.

A WINDING PATH CREATES
A GARDEN SURPRISE

I decided to begin, naturally enough, with my own 22- by 32-foot garden. Consisting of a central planting area surrounded on three sides by a walkway, the garden seemed static and two-dimensional. Everything was visible at once, and consequently it seemed smaller and more limited — not as interesting and inviting as I wanted it to be.

I thought that if the garden could unfold more gradually it would seem larger by providing those welcome elements of surprise and discovery that amplify the pleasures of a garden. I also realized that if I put the planting areas on the outer edges, with the living area toward the middle, I could generate more privacy and, at the same time, expand the planting area. This too would enhance the sense of spaciousness.

To do this, I built a bluestone path that wanders out from the door to the patio, canopied by two major planting groups on either side. I placed the patio more or less in the center of the yard, planting trees, shrubs, vines, and perennials on all four sides. Adjacent, I built a small fishpond and a stone-faced barbecue.

Now, as you enter the garden area, you get just a glimpse of the pond and a portion of the patio beyond, seen through the leafy overhang of trees and shrubs. It's only as you follow the winding path that the garden opens up. Stepping through the cascading foliage, you find yourself in a paved clearing, enveloped within leaves and flow-

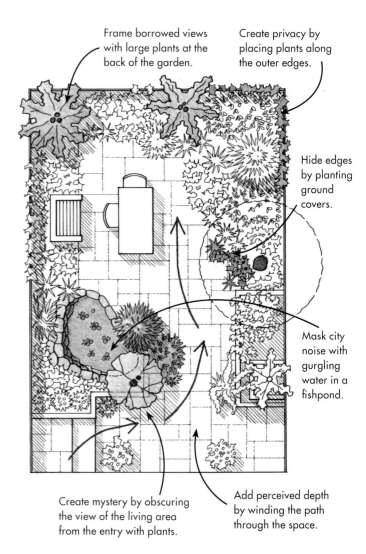

Frame borrowed views with large plants at the back of the garden.

Create privacy by placing plants along the outer edges.

Hide edges by planting ground covers.

Mask city noise with gurgling water in a fishpond.

Add perceived depth by winding the path through the space.

Create mystery by obscuring the view of the living area from the entry with plants.

ers. The impact is palpable. Once on the patio, the barbecue and dining table suggest their own possibilities, and the pond offers views of flashing fish and water lilies.

DIVIDING IS MORE LIKE MULTIPLYING

The next site I designed was also afflicted with what seemed like inherent limitations, although different from the ones in my own garden. Exposed as a fishbowl, barren, and narrow, this second lot appeared particularly uninviting and unusable.

To correct this problem, I created two distinctly separate spaces. Most people tend to think that a small area divided becomes smaller still. Yet if it's done with a sense of proportion and with enough room given to each area, dividing becomes more like multiplying—increasing the perception of space as well as possible experiences.

The dining area appears at the end of a bluestone path, enhancing its intimate feeling.

An arbor divides the two spaces of this garden, inviting visitors to venture beyond.

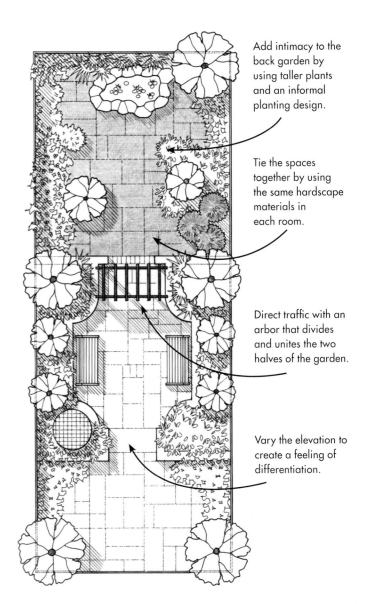

Add intimacy to the back garden by using taller plants and an informal planting design.

Tie the spaces together by using the same hardscape materials in each room.

Direct traffic with an arbor that divides and unites the two halves of the garden.

Vary the elevation to create a feeling of differentiation.

I made the first space the largest and ample enough for a variety of outdoor activities, thus eliminating any sense of confinement. The second space, visible through an arbor, invites you onward. When you step into this garden, you can't help but wonder what's back there.

To further enhance the sense of separation, I excavated the second area, dropping it several inches below the first. I also gave it an entirely different character from the front garden. The front area is formal in layout; it's symmetrical and made of bluestone with mortared joints and raised brick planters. The rear area, on the other hand, is free-form and informal. It too is paved with bluestone, but this time I laid it on top of the soil, with brick randomly worked in. The layout is irregular and the beds are ground level. The built-in sandbox, small water garden, and profusion of wildlife-attracting plants (for the birds, squirrels, butterflies, and dragonflies) enhance the casual atmosphere.

These garden areas are very different, yet together they create a unity, which is important in maintaining a sense of place. The arbor, for example, both joins the areas and separates them. It helps create a visual barrier while framing a view into the garden and beyond, serving to set each area apart while inviting the visitor from one area into the other.

The use of the same materials—like brick and stone—also helps tie the two areas together, as does the repetition of the more dramatic plants.

TERRACING ADDS DIMENSION TO A LONG, NARROW SPACE

Dividing by three works too. Another site I designed was about 80 feet by 20 feet—quite large by urban standards, yet it seemed tiny and inaccessible. Part of the problem was in the unfortunate division of space, achieved through the use of poorly placed trees. I decided to divide this long, narrow lot into three separate areas.

The area closest to the house features a redwood deck that flows easily down to an intimate patio that's accented by an informal water garden and graceful plantings. I separated this first space from the second one by installing a wide arbor that permits an easy view into the second and third garden areas. The second area is the largest and adds

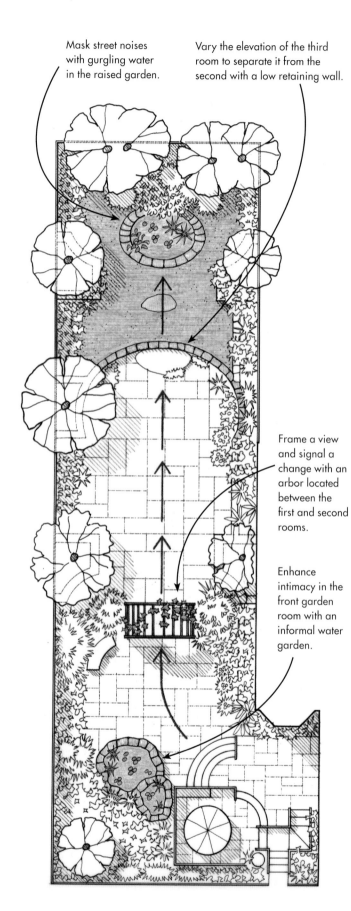

Mask street noises with gurgling water in the raised garden.

Vary the elevation of the third room to separate it from the second with a low retaining wall.

Frame a view and signal a change with an arbor located between the first and second rooms.

Enhance intimacy in the front garden room with an informal water garden.

A change in elevation can also signal a move from one area of the garden to another.

considerably to the yard's overall sense of spaciousness. You move from an intimate yet ample deck and patio area into a roomier area that offers a view into still another chamber of the garden. This experience of motion, of expansion through space, creates the illusion of vastness.

The third area is elevated and separated from the second area by a low stone wall. Proportion here is important. If too tall, the wall would have the effect of a barrier, inhibiting forward motion; if too low, it would seem foolish and unnecessary. As it is, the wall lifts the eye, carrying your vision into some remote point undeterminable because of the abundant plantings at the rear of the garden.

The semiformal water garden in the third area serves several functions. It sits like a jewel in its verdant surroundings, providing both visual and auditory interest as well as masking street noises. The water garden also serves as a focal point starting from the very front of the garden, where it draws your attention from the deck through the entire expanse of the landscape.

Although filled with diversity, these three spaces are welded into one environment by two primary elements—the use of stone and the repetition of form.

CURVES AND DIAGONALS ENLARGE A VIEW

Creating divisions and providing mystery are not the only ways to enlarge small spaces. Working with line is also important. Because the shortest distance between two points is a straight line—visually as well as physically—when everything in a small space is linear, we see everything at once. Our eyes don't traverse the length of the

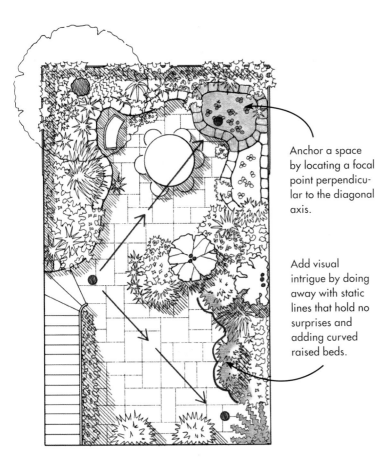

Anchor a space by locating a focal point perpendicular to the diagonal axis.

Add visual intrigue by doing away with static lines that hold no surprises and adding curved raised beds.

line but go immediately to the end, taking no joy in the journey. The space seems to shrink as we instantly see the whole garden at once.

Consider, for example, this urban landscape. It was a dark, flat, two-dimensional rectangle, utterly without interest. By building a curved wall that supports the raised beds and the water garden, I succeeded in doing away with that static, linear quality. Now, our attention is first swept along this curve but then it leaps away at various points to different views the garden offers (see the photo on p. 134).

Diagonal lines can be used for the same effect. For example, a patio laid diagonally to the length-width axis of a given area will pleasantly break up our customary axial orientation and help convey a greater sense of space. When using diagonals, I try to incorporate other elements within that orientation. I might, for instance, allow a portion of a retaining wall to sweep out and follow the diagonal lines of the patio for some distance. Or I may place an arbor perpendicular to the diagonal axis, thereby strengthening the diagonal focus and anchoring it within the total space.

WATER FEATURES PIQUE INTEREST

The use of details is valuable in adding depth and dimension to small spaces and such details can be included in a variety of ways. Any element that enhances our senses has the effect of expanding and prolonging our garden experience. Water gardens are ideal for this, and I've come to include them in many of my gardens. Consider the delightful sound of cascading water, reflections on a placid pool, the colors and motion of swimming fish, and day- and night-blooming water lilies. What other elements offer so much in so little space?

GARDENING
ON THE ROCKS

Even the rockiest terrain can be home to lush gardens by creating pockets of plants that work in tandem with nature. Gardeners Steve Biskey and Mark Watters reveal how they strung together a series of small rock gardens to make their garden flow despite the terrain.

WHEN WE BOUGHT A CABIN IN THE WOODS, WE WERE THRILLED about the prospect of surrounding our new home with a garden. We had fallen in love with the beauty of the exposed boulders on our land, but we soon discovered that the soil on the site was merely an inch or two of clay atop solid sandstone bedrock. Calling it "terra firma" would be a gross understatement. But, with perseverance and an open-minded attitude, we learned how to transform this inhospitable site into a thriving garden.

A site located on a bedrock ledge was transformed into a thriving garden by creating sequences of planting pockets. The authors linked their growing areas to form a continuous series of beds.

SUCCESSES AND FAILURES
LEAD TO DISCOVERY

We started our first garden in an area where the previous owners had constructed a 10-foot-square raised bed. After removing the bed's wooden frame and replacing it with gathered flat stone, we expanded its borders considerably and set out to plant. Oblivious to the fact that we were living on a huge expanse of rock, we gardened as we had done when we lived in the Midwest and Southwest. We chose perennials, planted them in our raised bed filled with new soil, added mulch, and then tended them.

As that first summer progressed, those perennials survived well enough. The following spring, however, we were faced with a near desert. Of the initial plantings, only some peonies (*Paeonia* spp. and cvs., USDA Hardiness Zones 3–8), a coreopsis (*Coreopsis verticillata* 'Moonbeam', Zones 3–8), and a rose of Sharon shrub (*Hibiscus syriacus* cv., Zones 5–9) had survived. We had no clue as to why some plants thrived and others did not. Over the next couple of years, we bought many more plants and nurtured each season's scraggly survivors as best we could. As the death toll climbed, we became more and more determined to figure out a way to coax our plantings to grow.

Our gardening efforts took a turn for the better when we decided to plant a tree in memory of our dear friend Gerda, who had died. Coincidentally, we were in the process of removing an old, long-unused outhouse, which stood in an area we intended to turn into a garden. Upon removing the structure, we were thrilled to discover it had been built above a fissure between two boulders that was 5 to 6 feet deep and about 3 feet wide. This would become our first large planting hole. We filled this large crevice with new soil that we mixed from topsoil, sand, and aged horse manure. Then we planted a Washington hawthorn (*Crataegus phaenopyrum*, Zones 4–8). To our delight, the tree thrived.

With this success, we began to analyze this crevice, following its lines to see where it went, in hopes of finding additional deep planting areas. We began to see that all the naturally occurring plants were living along these crevices. These clefts in the rock ledge measured anywhere from a few inches to several feet deep and wide. Upon further investigation, we realized that the bedrock outcroppings naturally sloped toward these crevices, depositing rainwater and nutrients there.

Armed with our new awareness, we went back to our original raised bed and shoveled the soil away from the bedrock, exposing the crevices as we went. In doing so, we discovered that our own few surviving plants had thrived because we had inadvertently placed them in or near crevices.

Inspired by these insights, our approach to gardening took a new direction. After removing the weedy mass from atop a crevice, we used hand shovels, pry bars, and our bare hands to remove the soil, gravel, and rocks that filled the fissure. Depending on the depth of an empty crevice, we sometimes used some of the rocks to backfill the area and provide drainage. Then we filled the crevice with soil and planted.

After clearing out the space between two boulders, refill the fissure with good soil and plants.

Planting pockets within a large crevice combine with an informal path material to maintain a natural feel.

Astilbes, hostas, and other shade plants are among the many plants that thrive within soil pockets on this rocky site.

SEVEN EASY STEPS TO MAKING SOIL

In her book *Lasagna Gardening*, Patricia Lanza describes a well-organized system of layering organic materials to make soil. We tend to make our "lasagna" soil more informally. Although the following steps are outlined in sequence, this method works for us even if we skip some of the later steps or vary the sequence a bit. The process usually takes at least a year to complete.

1 Smother any sod or weeds in a new garden area by placing several layers of wet newspaper on the ground.

2 Cover the area with grass cuttings, plant prunings, and weeding remnants. If you want to include small twigs and branches, cut them into 3- to 4-inch sections and scatter them evenly over the area. Over time, add kitchen scraps, including fruit and vegetable leftovers, coffee grounds and filters, eggshells, and used paper towels. (Do not include meat products since they attract animals.)

3 When you have a fairly thick and uniform layer of material to be composted—2 to 3 inches deep—add a 2- to 3-inch layer of manure or already composted organic matter.

4 Add a 2- to 3-inch layer of peat moss.

5 Repeat steps 2, 3, and 4 until the layers measure 10 to 12 inches high.

6 During fall cleanup, add a layer of shredded leaves. (Unshredded leaves will also work, but they decompose more slowly.) The soil and plants from potted annuals can also be spread evenly as a layer of the "lasagna."

7 To hasten the composting process, cover the layers with wet newspaper and mulch, such as rough wood chips. There's no need to turn or stir the layers. Monitor the decomposition process, and begin to plant when the materials have reached the crumbly texture of loamy soil, after a year or so.

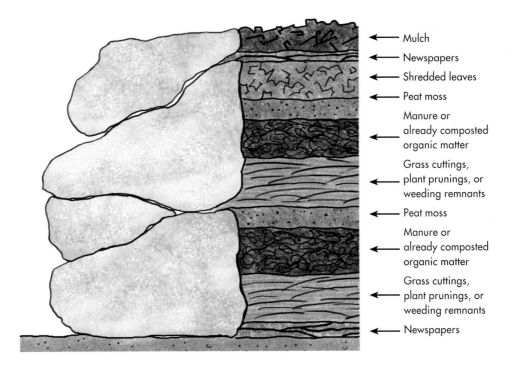

← Mulch

← Newspapers

← Shredded leaves

← Peat moss

← Manure or already composted organic matter

← Grass cuttings, plant prunings, or weeding remnants

← Peat moss

← Manure or already composted organic matter

← Grass cuttings, plant prunings, or weeding remnants

← Newspapers

RAISED BEDS ADD MORE AREAS FOR PLANTINGS

In addition to taking advantage of the depth that the excavated crevices provided, we also created extra raised beds by using flat stones to build up the soil level surrounding a crevice area (see the photo at left). By doing so, we were able to extend the size of planting areas while taking advantage of the increased soil depth.

Since there was very little soil on our site, we filled every planting area with soil we made ourselves. A nearby horse farm provided us with truckloads of old, ripe manure, and we bought topsoil, sand, and other materials to round out the mix. Making each batch of soil and hauling it over the rocky, multilevel landscape did, however, take its toll on us. We were going broke buying the ingredients and were getting too old to haul soil all day. To remedy this, we decided to try a method of on-site composting we discovered in a book (see the sidebar on p. 145).

All of our efforts paid off. Our plants were well nourished and grew vigorously. To increase our odds of succeeding, we invariably chose plants that we knew were fairly tough. Eventually, we connected separate planting beds into a continuous garden linked by paths.

Turning our rocky site into a lush garden has been a rewarding but slow process over the past 17 years rather than an overnight transformation. By observing and working with the attributes of our site, we have continually evolved our gardening techniques. We recognize that in making this garden we are truly in a partnership with nature.

A simple way to increase soil depth is to create raised beds with layered flat stones.

Even within the limits of the rocky terrain, you can create garden rooms for entertaining or relaxing.

PLANTING
ON A SLOPE

A typical retaining wall isn't your only option for making room to plant and room to play. Garden designer Erin Ray shows you how to incorporate a slope into your overall garden design—and still have a usable space.

MANY OF THE HOUSES IN THE PORTLAND, OREGON, neighborhood in which my husband and I live rest on lots that are higher than the street. Erecting 4- to 5-foot-high retaining walls made out of stone, brick, or concrete is a common solution for dealing with these sloping lots. In most cases, these walls are placed right at the sidewalk to create a nice, level front yard— easy to mow, easy to maintain. Though this is a practical approach to the challenges presented by gardening on a slope, it's not the only answer.

Our lot has two large elevation changes to consider: one street side and the other in the backyard. When we purchased the home, the front landscape incorporated a rock retaining wall, while the

In front, large planting pockets are key. They allow for flexibility in plant choice, resulting in a lively area full of unique plants in various sizes, shapes, and colors.

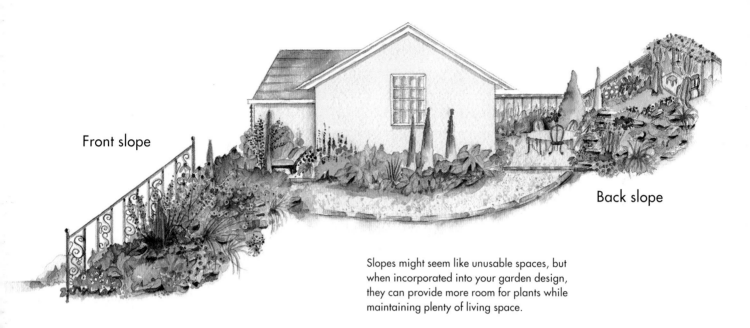

Front slope

Back slope

Slopes might seem like unusable spaces, but when incorporated into your garden design, they can provide more room for plants while maintaining plenty of living space.

back slope used two brick terraces; both types of structures had a certain charm that complemented our Cape Cod–style home, but neither displayed the creative style I had in mind. With my love of gardening and our wish for plenty of level, usable living space, two new retaining walls would have been a logical choice. But typical retaining walls weren't part of our vision. We wanted something functional yet unique. With careful thought given to how we wanted each slope to work for us, we designed them to be an integral part of our garden, not just a way to retain it.

GO VERTICAL TO INCREASE YOUR LIVING SPACE

We decided to tackle the back slope first, mainly because the two original brick terraces were falling apart. In replacing the old terraces, we were determined to preserve as much level ground as possible at the bottom and top of the slope. Our design choice was to build one rock wall with a nearly vertical rise, similar to the original wall in front but with a twist: adding small planting pockets between the rocks. This layout provides room at the base of the slope for cooking and dining on our patio; space up top for gardening, relaxing, and playing with our dog; and additional space for planting between the rocks.

To achieve this nearly vertical slope, we stacked boulders practically on top of each other, leaving small planting pockets between the rocks. When planted, these pockets transform the slope into a beautiful living wall—a spectacular backdrop for the lower patio (see the bottom photo on p. 152). Chunky stone stairs complement the rocky slope and provide access to the upper garden, while two columnar 'Wilma Goldcrest' cypress (*Cupressus macrocarpa* 'Wilma Goldcrest, USDA Hardiness Zones 7–11) on either side of the top step mark the entrance to this level (see the top photo on p. 153). Visually, it's a natural way to make the transition—though adding a subtle handrail would make it easier for everyone to use the stairs, especially at night.

With this living wall in place, we accomplished our main goal of maximizing the living space. The design has produced some challenges, however. The planting pockets between the boulders are hospitable only to certain plants, and the ones that are happiest there tend to take over. Every few years, I play referee by removing oregano (*Origanum* spp. and cvs., Zones 4–9), crocosmia (*Crocosmia* spp. and cvs., Zones 6–9), asters (*Aster* spp. and cvs., Zones 4–8), and other spreaders, while adding various evergreens, perennials, and annuals to achieve the look I want.

A true nature scene needs water. This small water feature built into our back slope provides soothing background noise and adds an extra element of interest to the design.

Plants make the difference. Without lush, fully grown plantings, our back slope is a plain gray-brown backdrop of rock (above). Once the plants fill in, however, the rocks fade into the background, and we're presented with a vibrant, colorful living wall (below).

Erosion is another issue. As an organic gardener, I bring in compost to feed my plants every year. The only way to add it to the back slope is to press it in, a handful at a time, yet some of it still runs off with rain or watering. These challenges were something we wanted to avoid once we moved on to redesigning the front slope.

MAXIMIZE THE SLOPE FOR MORE PLANTING

After more than 10 years of gardening on the rebuilt back slope and the original front slope—a lawn gradually descending away from the house to an almost vertical rock retaining wall ranging from 4 to 5 feet high—we finally tackled the redesign of our front yard. We knew we wanted an attractive way to get to the front door with plenty of room for plants, a nice place to sit and relax, and no more

AFTER

sloping lawn to mow. We also wanted to avoid the plant limitations and drainage issues of the back slope.

By laying tracing paper over a photo of the existing wall, I drew a sketch to convey my idea: large, level planting spaces between big boulders that retain the slope, with a seating area at the top. We teamed up with a local stone mason and contractor to complete the design.

By replacing the original retaining wall with a progression of carefully placed boulders to secure the slope, our contractor brought my vision to life. He sited the boulders to look as if they had arrived there naturally. The lower ones support the upper ones while also maximizing the height gained behind each boulder without taking up a lot of horizontal space. The increase in height created by the placement of the boulders allows more room for large horizontal planting areas while still leaving room up top for a level seating area.

To make the slope accessible, we kept the preexisting concrete stairs, adding a bluestone landing (which matches the new patio) with two more stone stairs to get to the newly created level area at the top. Brick risers were incorporated into the new stairs to tie them in with the brick used for the original front-door stoop. An artistic stair railing adds interest, and a trio of Tiny Tower® Italian cypress (*Cupressus sempervirens* 'Monshel', Zones 7–10) alternate along each side of the front stairs and lead to the front door (see the photo on p. 154).

ABOVE Use stone to achieve a natural look. Concrete or brick stairs would really stand out against this thickly planted rock wall. Stone stairs, however, add just the right complementary touch.

LEFT A blank slate can be intimidating. But keeping your plant palette small and visualizing how each plant will function best in the landscape makes it easier to tackle the task.

With no more lawn to mow, the homeowners can enjoy the view from the new front terrace.

The new front slope's large, level planting spaces address a number of the difficulties we have with the back slope, the most important of which is that I'm not limited to the same small-size, drought-tolerant rock-garden plants that I often have to use in the back. I make my plant choices based on the full-sun, south-facing orientation, picking plants for year-round interest and low maintenance. Repeating a small selection of plants that meet these criteria gives a cohesive look to the entire wall while keeping maintenance to a minimum. Large plants, like 'Fernspray Gold' hinoki cypress (*Chamaecyparis obtusa* 'Fernspray Gold', Zones 4–8) and 'Royal Purple' smoke tree (*Cotinus coggygria* 'Royal Purple', Zones 5-9), are planted in the largest level areas between rocks, while grasses and other perennials are planted in smaller spaces and sloped areas. After working around the boulders, my plantings loosely follow a triangular design, with struc-

tural plants spread across the wall and smaller plants grouped together.

The erosion issues we face with the back slope are not a concern on our new front slope. We use drip irrigation to get water directly to the plants, and even with plenty of rain, the level areas between the boulders help prevent erosion, while ground covers, like woolly thyme (*Thymus pseudolanuginosus*, Zones 5–9) and hens and chicks (*Sempervivum* spp. and cvs., Zones 4–11), do their magic to secure soil and mulch. Now that the work is complete on the back and front slopes, I love sitting on the front patio enjoying a glass of wine and conversation with friends while being just visible enough to entice a passing neighbor to stop and join us. Even with all the challenges that gardening on a slope presents, the result is well worth the effort with the right design in place.

DEALING WITH DRAINAGE

The back slope of our property was where we began our experiment with drainage. At the base of the slope, we installed a French drain to prevent the patio—and eventually our basement—from flooding during a heavy rain. This drain was the simplest solution and solved the problem. Although the front slope doesn't have the runoff issues we have in the back, the new design gave us a chance to play with a different kind of drainage. We disconnected the roof downspout that drained rainwater into the sewer, and that water is now absorbed on-site. According to the city of Portland, disconnecting all or part of your roof drain system is a simple, environmentally sound solution to the city's combined sewer overflow problem.

ABOVE A rain chain hangs from the gutter of our home, draining rainwater into an urn that empties into a drainage pipe running under the patio, down to the front slope, onto a large basin-shaped basalt rock, and into two awaiting dry wells that collect it.

LEFT Dry wells slowly release water belowground, preventing it from reaching the storm drains. Drainage pipes and wells are covered aboveground by a dry streambed of colorful stones.

A pleasant means to an end: Irregularly shaped stepping-stones encourage visitors to slow down and enjoy the journey in this garden passageway between the busy street and a peaceful backyard retreat.

MAKE THE MOST
OF EVERY SQUARE FOOT

Don't write off a narrow side yard. This transitional space can—and should—be a destination in its own right. Landscape designer Scott Endres shows you how he created beauty in his own small space.

WHEN I MOVED INTO MY HOME 12 YEARS AGO, I FELT constricted by the amount of space available for gardening. My humble 40- by 80-foot lot was monopolized by my 1889 Victorian house, with a small front yard, a tiny backyard, and a narrow side yard. I knew I would have to make the most of every square inch of space. The front and back were no-brainers: The front would be a public space with bold plantings to be viewed from the street and sidewalk; the backyard would become a private oasis, a retreat from the hustle and bustle of everyday life.

The side garden would be more challenging. I wanted this garden to be an experience, not just an expressway between the front and the back. Besides, I needed more space for plantings, and I wanted to enjoy this space as much as the other areas. My job was to broaden the space psychologically and make it into a destination that would tempt guests to linger as they passed from the public to the private areas of my garden. Success would rely on wise hardscape decisions, the careful placement of plants and focal points, and the inventive use of repetition to pull it all together.

HARDSCAPE DEFINES THE SPACE

Although I needed to enclose the space, I couldn't bear the idea of a tall, solid privacy fence. It would make the already narrow space feel claustrophobic and would shade the garden from the precious southern sun. A hedge would take up too much real estate. I opted instead for a decorative period-style cast-iron fence to border the side garden, transitioning to a taller wooden privacy fence that would surround the private back garden. The iron fence fits the architecture of the house, and the visual weight of the fence is enough to define the space without closing it off from the outside.

I chose an irregular stone path to lead visitors through the garden. Although they create a straight line, the irregularly shaped stones slow traffic and invite one to experience every step of the journey.

PLANTINGS AND FOCAL POINTS CONTROL VIEWS

This part of the garden is a transition between rooms, a prelude to the restful back garden or a memorable exit for my guests. For those entering the garden, I placed a large pottery jardiniere at the end of the path to point toward the final destination and signal the beginning of a new experience in the back garden. The front gate indicates the opposite destination for guests leaving the garden. Taller plantings and more trees and shrubs at either end of the garden also hint at the transition from this side room into the front or back by blocking the views between rooms.

I already had seating areas on the front porch and back patio, so I found no need to include more on the side. I wanted the space to be taken in from the path, which gives a unique perspective by allowing one to see the long view of the garden as a whole and then to appreciate the intricacies of the individual plantings along the way. These plantings serve as visual resting areas as they catch the eye. I also kept art and statuary to a minimum in this garden. Too much would have muddled the experience, and I wanted the plants to be the stars.

In this garden, I keep in mind how each plant and combination works within the garden as a whole when viewed from the path. Repetition of colors, forms, or, in some cases, plant varieties ties it all together, connecting front and back, left and right, while directing the viewer's eye through the garden. I repeat, for example, chartreuse

ABOVE Two fences serve two purposes. An open fence, which keeps the passageway open and breezy, transitions to a solid fence toward the back of the space, where more privacy is desired.

plants throughout the garden. The bright foliage of a golden Korean fir (*Abies koreana* 'Aurea', USDA Hardiness Zones 5–6) is followed by two groupings of 'Lime Glow' creeping juniper (*Juniperus horizontalis* 'Lime Glow', Zones 3–9) and then a trio of golden 'Mops' sawara cypress (*Chamacyparis pisifera* 'Mops', Zones 4–8). The bright color is inviting, and its repetition draws visitors down the path, step by step. I try to alternate these groupings on either side of the path to give equal merit to both sides and to trick the eye to slow down and take in as much as possible.

Plant forms can do this too. The vertical form of variegated iris (*Iris pallida* 'Albo-marginata', Zones 4–9) is repeated with groups of 'Karl Foerster' feather reed grass (*Calamagrostis* × *acutiflora* 'Karl Foerster', Zones 5–9) and 'Helmond Pillar' Japanese barberry (*Berberis thunbergii* 'Hellmond Pillar', Zones 5–8) in other parts of the garden. This repetition creates a consistent harmony as one's eye picks up familiar notes along the way. I avoid the "runway" feeling that a straight path can have by repeating the same plant on either side of the walkway. A small group of variegated iris at the beginning of the path is repeated with a bigger group on the other side, connecting the two sides. Groupings of bergenia (*Bergenia cordifolia*, Zones 3–8), 'Mops' sawara cypress, and 'Elijah Blue' blue fescue (*Festuca glauca* 'Elijah Blue', Zones 4–8) do the same thing at other points along the way.

My efforts in this garden have made this narrow passageway an integral part of my garden, one that can stand on its own while also serving its purpose. With careful attention to detail, the side yard is no longer an afterthought but rather an important transitional space that's a prelude to my inner sanctum and an extension of my home and personality.

At the end of the path, visitors are rewarded with this exciting space that is an extension of the author's home and personality.

SEVEN ELEMENTS OF A SUCCESSFUL PASSAGEWAY

This narrow side yard uses several devices to create a transitional space that also provides its own unique experience.

1 An open, iron fence keeps the passageway from feeling closed in.

2 A solid fence begins toward the back of the space for more privacy.

3 Irregular stepping-stones require visitors to slow down, which gives them time to look around.

4 Taller plantings serve as visual barriers and signal that the path is almost at its end.

5 A large planter at the end of the walkway serves as a focal point.

6 Staggered repetition of colors, forms, and plants connects both sides of the path and keeps the eye looking forward.

7 The destination is a soothing and lovely patio, a worthy culmination of this journey.

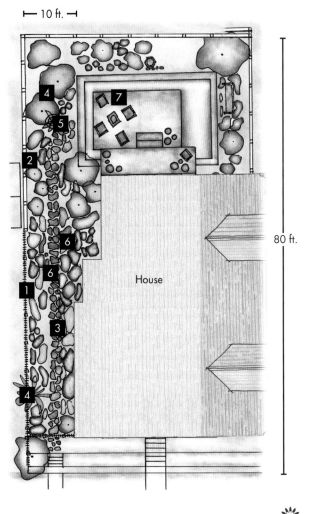

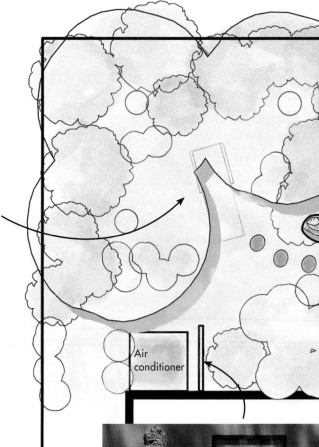

TIPS FOR BREAKING UP THE BACKYARD BOX

As lot sizes continue to shrink, long and narrow backyards are fast becoming the standard in suburbs everywhere. Add a typical 6-foot-tall fence separating you from your neighbors and it's easy to feel like you're living in a box instead of a garden. Throw in the challenge of finding room for all of the activities you enjoy—whether it's dining alfresco, relaxing with a book, or puttering in the garden—and it's clear a traditional square patio surrounded by lawn and shrubs just won't get the job done. You might think that breaking up the open rectangular space would make it feel even smaller; but in reality, planting between the lines adds depth and interest, making the garden feel bigger than it is.

Air conditioner

Make each defined area feel cozy by weaving planting beds throughout the garden instead of just planting along the fence perimeter. While it's seldom practical in a small garden to completely separate one space from another, a series of connected nooks partially separated by plants creates a delightful sense of mystery and discovery and results in a garden that is both intimate and integrated.

Art has a purpose. A colorful privacy screen hides an air conditioner and makes an attractive focal point.

In a small space, the shape of the patio is one of the most important design elements, and a gracefully curving patio is an excellent way to soften hard edges. A patio with a double curve has the added benefit of creating two slightly separated areas, further de-emphasizing the feeling of one long, continuous space. If you add a table for dining on one side and a comfortable spot for lounging on the other, you will have two garden destinations.

To make your space seem even bigger, lay tiles or pavers on the diagonal. If your patio will be made out of concrete, have your installer cut the score lines on a diagonal at 5-foot intervals.

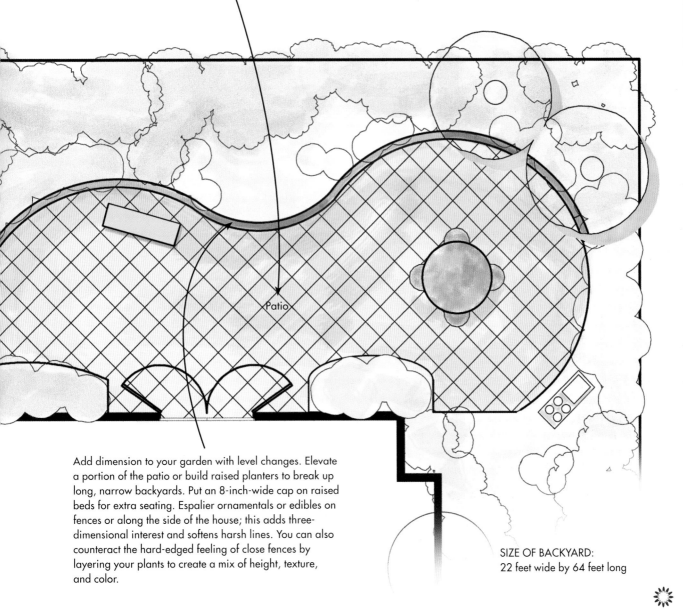

Patio

Add dimension to your garden with level changes. Elevate a portion of the patio or build raised planters to break up long, narrow backyards. Put an 8-inch-wide cap on raised beds for extra seating. Espalier ornamentals or edibles on fences or along the side of the house; this adds three-dimensional interest and softens harsh lines. You can also counteract the hard-edged feeling of close fences by layering your plants to create a mix of height, texture, and color.

SIZE OF BACKYARD:
22 feet wide by 64 feet long

A pyramidal dwarf Alberta spruce (right) and two golden Eastern arborvitae (center and left) provide year-round structure in a front garden.

DESIGNING WITH
DWARF CONIFERS

Even small spaces benefit from adding conifers. Not only do they add year-round interest, but they also bring structure and height to the garden. These tips from horticulture teacher Melinda Myers help you fit them in and still leave you with room to grow.

WHEN I STARTED TO GARDEN, I INITIALLY GOT HOOKED ON perennials. To make room for as many as possible in my small city lot, I got rid of my front-yard patch of grass and began planting. My entry garden was soon a showcase of color and texture from spring to fall. But something was missing. My garden needed more of a framework, including some vertical accents and year-round plantings.

My tiny lot did not afford much space for full-size trees and shrubs, but I knew I could make room for a few dwarf conifers, which usually don't get taller than 1 to 6 feet in 10 years. Adding some conifers to the mix turned out to be the perfect solution.

Dwarf conifers can serve as versatile plants regardless of how much space you have. Three key ways to use them are as anchors of ever-changing planting vignettes, as vertical elements in a design, and in clusters with other dwarf conifers.

The selection of dwarf conifers available to home gardeners has greatly increased in the past decade. You can find them in shades of green, blue, and yellow and in variegated colors. I find helpful to choose a conifer based on its color and its habit, whether upright, mounding, or pyramidal (see the chart on the facing page).

Although it may seem more daunting to purchase and plant a conifer than a perennial, don't be afraid to make mistakes. Fortunately, the small size and slow-growth habit of dwarf conifers make them easier to transplant than some woody plants. In fact, gardeners considering a move within 10 years of planting a dwarf conifer would likely be able to pack it up along with their favorite perennials, roses, and household belongings.

USE SMALL CONIFERS TO ANCHOR CHANGING VIGNETTES

I think of dwarf conifers as garden stalwarts. One way to capitalize on these evergreens is to make them anchors in mixed plantings that change from season to season. Compact evergreens provide attractive stability in a bed or border as bulbs, perennials, and annuals come and go. Conifers with all types of contours, from low mounds to pyramids, can be used in this way.

A planting with year-round appeal is a great way to enhance the entrance to your home. Two avid gardeners I know in Milwaukee, Steve Bialk and Angela Duckert, created just that. A dwarf Alberta spruce (*Picea glauca* var. *albertiana* 'Conica', USDA Hardiness Zones 2–6) serves as the central figure in their front-yard vignette, providing soft texture and a pyramidal shape that balance the low heft of a large boulder (see the photo on p. 162). In summer, the bold, blue-green leaves of a *Hosta* cultivar (Zones 3–9) contrast with the spruce's fine needles. Two golden Eastern arborvitae (*Thuja occidentalis* 'Sunkist', Zones 4–7)

ABOVE Two dwarf golden Eastern arborvitae and a blue juniper create a textural vignette with a cotoneaster.

LEFT A creeping blue juniper cascades on a rocky slope and serves as a centerpiece among seasonally changing plantings.

OUTSTANDING DWARF CONIFERS

In general, these plants grow in average, well-drained garden soil and full sun. The plants are grouped by mature form, and the height refers to the mature height at 10 years.

NAME	ZONES	HEIGHT
GLOBELIKE		
DWARF MUGO PINE (*Pinus mugo* 'Mops')	3–7	2 feet
GOLDEN EASTERN ARBORVITAE (*Thuja occidentalis* 'Rheingold')	2–7	3 feet
GOLDEN MUGO PINE (*Pinus mugo* 'Aurea')	3–7	3 feet
MOUNDING		
DWARF GOLDEN THREADLEAF SAWARA CYPRESS (*Chamaecyparis pisifera* 'Filifera Aurea Nana')	4–8	3 feet
'GOLDEN MOP' SAWARA CYPRESS (*Chamaecyparis pisifera* 'Golden Mop', also called 'Mops')	4–8	2 to 3 feet
'SHERWOOD COMPACT' MUGO PINE (*Pinus mugo* 'Sherwood Compact')	3–7	2 feet
THREADLEAF VARIEGATED SAWARA CYPRESS (*Chamaecyparis pisifera* 'Filifera Aureovariegata')	4–8	3 feet
PYRAMIDAL		
DWARF ALBERTA SPRUCE (*Picea glauca* var. *albertiana* 'Conica')	2–6	3½ feet
DWARF BLUE SPRUCE (*Picea pungens* 'Montgomery')	2–8	3 feet
DWARF EASTERN ARBORVITAE (*Thuja occidentalis* 'Holmstrup')	2–7	3 feet
DWARF PYRAMIDAL HINOKI CYPRESS (*Chamaecyparis obtusa* 'Nana Gracilis')	4–8	3 feet
'GENTSCH'S WHITE' HEMLOCK (*Tsuga canadensis* 'Gentsch's White')	4–8	3 feet
GOLDEN EASTERN ARBORVITAE (*Thuja occidentalis* 'Sunkist')	4–7	4 feet
'RAINBOW'S END' WHITE SPRUCE (*Picea glauca* 'Rainbow's End')	2–6	4 feet
'SANDER'S BLUE' WHITE SPRUCE (*Picea glauca* 'Sander's Blue')	2–6	3 feet
'TECHNITO' ARBORVITAE (*Thuja occidentalis* 'Technito')	3–7	4 feet
SPREADING		
BIRD'S NEST SPRUCE (*Picea abies* 'Nidiformis')	3–8	3 feet
DWARF NORWAY SPRUCE (*Picea abies* 'Elegans')	3–8	3 feet
'ICEE BLUE' CREEPING JUNIPER (*Juniperus horizontalis* 'Icee Blue')	3–9	4 inches
PROSTRATE CANADIAN HEMLOCK (*Tsuga canadensis* 'Cole's Prostrate')	4–8	2½ feet

and a low-growing juniper round out the scene. Behind the spruce, a variegated miscanthus (*Miscanthus sinensis* 'Variegatus', Zones 6–9) adds a bright accent with its narrow-striped leaves, which repeat the variegation of a deadnettle (*Lamium maculat*um cv., Zones 4–8). In fall, the hosta turns a beautiful yellow, echoing the color of the arborvitae foliage. The evergreens continue to add colorful structure in winter.

In another mixed planting, a dwarf mugo pine (*Pinus mugo* ssp. *mugo*, Zones 3–7), a 'Rheingold' arborvitae (*Thuja occidentalis* 'Rheingold', Zones 2–7), and a daylily (*Hemerocallis* cv., Zones 3–10) create an appealing vignette. The green needles of the mugo pine contrast with the color and texture of the apricot-tinged arborvitae. The arborvitae foliage forms a pleasing color harmony with the melon-colored daylily blossoms. The planting is completed by a skirt of the foliage of a bigroot geranium (*Geranium macrorrhizum*, Zones 4–8).

Dwarf conifers also mix well with roses and deciduous shrubs. In another part of this yard, an established dwarf blue spruce (*Picea pungens* 'Montgomery', Zones 2–8) serves as the steadfast element of a mixed planting along the corner of a slope (see the top photo above). A dwarf

Norway spruce (*Picea abies* 'Mucronata', Zones 3–8) adds textural contrast next to a hardy shrub rose that blooms throughout the summer. The rose's attractive hips add to the winter interest provided by the conifers. A yellow barberry (*Berberis thunbergii* cv., Zones 5–8) contrasts with the blue spruce and harmonizes with the chartreuse blooms of lady's mantle. Hostas, daylilies, and other perennials provide interesting foliage and seasonal blooms.

DWARF CONIFERS CAN ADD VERTICALITY

A common challenge that gardeners face is finding plants that add height without taking up a lot of space. A dwarf conifer with either a vertical, narrow habit or a pyramidal form can lend height to a combination, serve as a focal point, or add a sense of depth to a small or narrow bed. Good candidates for this type of design include upright and narrow arborvitae, false cypresses, and junipers. Pyramidal candidates include dwarf Alberta spruce and 'Technito' arborvitae (*Thuja occidentalis* 'Technito', Zones 3–7), a recently introduced smaller version of 'Techny' arborvitae.

As you walk through the Bialk-Duckert yard, the vertical structure provided by dwarf blue spruces and arborvitae helps unify the garden while expanding the sense of space (see the bottom photo on the facing page). At one corner of the lot, dwarf conifers provide vertical accents that soften the horizontal impact of a rock wall by creating a sense of scale and balance. An upright, intermediate arborvitae (*T. occidentalis* 'Yellow Ribbon', Zones 2–7), with intriguing swirls of golden foliage, and a pyramidal dwarf Alberta spruce serve as a visual bridge between mounds of perennials and towering trees in the background.

In another area of this garden, a backdrop planting of dwarf Alberta spruce draws attention from a hosta and astilbes in the foreground to create a pleasing sense of depth. The vertical backdrop of trees also helps muffle city noise and blocks the view of nearby buildings.

CLUSTER CONIFERS FOR IMPACT

In addition to enhancing mixed plantings, small conifers can be grouped with other conifers in eye-catching ways. A simple combination of two dwarf conifers, such as a 'Fat Albert' blue spruce (*Picea pungens* 'Fat Albert', Zones 2–8) and a 'Golden Mop' sawara cypress (*Chamaecyparis pisifera* 'Golden Mop', Zones 4–8), looks more dynamic than a few sheared yews lined up against a house foundation. In a garden with more space, use dwarf conifers to dress up an existing planting of evergreens. Dwarf and intermediate conifers can add color, form, and texture to an otherwise monotonous windbreak of tall conifers such as Colorado spruce and Austrian pines.

You can also enliven a serviceable evergreen hedge with a colorful companion or two. The broader, branching form of a 'Montgomery' blue spruce (*Picea pungens* 'Montgomery', Zones 2–8) contrasts nicely with the narrowly upright forms of an array of arborvitae.

One of my favorite conifer groupings is what I call "Rich's Gnome Forest." Rich Eyre planted about 20 green and blue dwarf Alberta spruces close together to create a small-scale forest at his nursery, Rich's Foxwillow Pines Nursery, in Woodstock, Illinois. One of his customers liked the planting enough to emulate it in his own landscape (see the photo below). Surrounded by a ground cover of creeping sedums, this miniature forest always gets a second look from visitors.

Dwarf conifers can be used to control erosion and eliminate the need to mow on a steep slope. Combined with a few weed-suppressing ground covers, a planting of several dwarf conifers can serve as an attractive and low-maintenance design solution.

Whether you have a large yard or a postage-stamp city lot, I'll bet you can find space for a few dwarf conifers. I certainly have—about eight and counting. My 'Gentsch's White' hemlock (*Tsuga canadensis* 'Gentsch's White', Zones 4–8) adds a vertical accent, and its white-tipped foliage brightens a corner of my shade garden. A bird's nest spruce (*Picea abies* 'Nidiformis', Zones 3–8) provides a year-round anchor for a small grouping of brunnera (*Brunnera macrophylla*, Zones 3–7), tulips, and annual pentas (*Pentas* cvs.) near my 'Candymint' crab apple (*Malus* 'Candymint', Zones 4–8). And the opportunities to include dwarf conifers grow as my garden evolves. You may find, as I have, that your garden will feel richer for their presence.

A grouping of dwarf Alberta spruces creates the effect of a miniature forest.

✓ **CONTAINER GARDEN**
✓ **PLANT SUGGESTIONS**
✓ **HOW-TO**

A WATER GARDEN TO FIT
ANY SPACE

A water garden in a container is an easy way to add new plants to your palette. Gardening author Greg Speichert gets you started by offering advice for the best plants to use and basic care tips.

FEW THINGS ARE CERTAIN WHEN IT COMES TO GARDENING. A sun-loving plant will do poorly in shade. An agave won't survive a Minnesota winter. Deer will eat your hostas. Here is another one: Water improves a garden. I'm not talking about giving your plants a drink (although that is true too). I'm referring to ponds and water features.

Water in the garden never goes unnoticed. Adding a water feature to a garden room or patio instantly creates a peaceful feeling and says that there is something special and distinct about the place. Water brings the light down from the sky and reflects it back to us. It heightens plants' textures and enhances their forms. Best of all, it opens up a new world of plants for us to grow. But who wants to excavate for a pond or run electricity for a pump and filter? Adding a water feature to your garden usually takes time, money, and effort.

If you have something that holds water, like this old kettle drum, you can have a water garden.

WATER CONTAINER BASICS

You don't need a fancy pump or a big system to have a container water garden, but you do need to do the basics correctly to have success. Here's what you need to know.

CHOOSING THE CONTAINER

While any container that holds water can become a water container, choose one with a suitable depth for the plants you will be growing. Use the size of your largest plant as a guide, and make sure that the container can provide the right depth. Smaller plants can be set on stones or bricks to raise them up.

If your perfect container has a hole in the bottom, put tape across the bottom of the hole, then plug the hole from the inside with plumber's putty (see the photo below). A container made from a porous material like terra-cotta will need to have a sealant applied before it will hold water.

SURVIVING WITHOUT A PUMP

Container water gardens hold a small amount of water, so in the unlikely event you get algae or mosquitoes, just dump out the container and add fresh water. Or you can simply overflow the container every time you add water, removing anything growing on or near the surface. Stagnancy shouldn't be a concern because the water is constantly being refreshed due to evaporation and plant use.

PLANTING TECHNIQUE

Place plants in the container, keeping them in their original pots. If the pots do not have a top layer of pea gravel, add one to prevent soil leakage, which would dirty the water. Be sure to set plants at the proper depth as you arrange them.

FEEDING THE PLANTS

I use a fertilizer intended for water plants because conditions underwater are different from those underground. I feed my plants monthly until the water reaches about 80°F, and then I fertilize every two weeks.

You can use a container even if it has a drainage hole. Just plug it with putty.

The solution is a water container. Find any object that can hold water and fill it up. You have just created an environment that will do all the wonderful things water does for a garden. Once you've set up a container (see the sidebar on the facing page), all that is left is the fun part: choosing the plants.

As with any container combination, water containers need a mixture of upright, bushy, and creeping plants to look balanced. The plants I have chosen to write about fit into these categories and can be combined with one another to create beautiful compositions. Each plant also has a stature and habit that work well in a container environment. These plants are available at any local nursery with a decent water gardening section, and they shouldn't cost any more than other perennials. Most are easily overwintered indoors, or you can grow them as annuals, tossing them onto the compost pile at season's end. While these plants are perfect for your first foray into the world of water garden plants, don't limit yourself to this small group. There is a wide palette of water plants for you to explore.

DWARF UMBRELLA GRASSES

Umbrella grasses (*Cyperus alternifolius* and cvs., syn. *C. involucratus*, USDA Hardiness Zones 9–11) usually grow up to 6 feet tall, but several dwarf cultivars are perfect for water containers. Their upright habit and long, narrow leaves add height and grace to a composition. 'Gracilis' retains the elegance of its taller cousins while reaching only 2 feet high and 1 foot wide. 'Variegatus' is as tall as 'Gracilis' but is twice as wide. As its name suggests, 'Variegatus' has striking green-and-white variegated leaves, but they often suddenly revert to all green. 'Nanus', which grows from 2 to 4 feet tall, is the biggest of the umbrella grasses I would recommend for a container.

Dwarf umbrella grasses are naturally yellow-green. The more sun they get, the more yellow their leaves become, especially if you don't feed the plant enough. If you want to be sure a plant stays green, give it morning sun and fertilize it regularly. Since dwarf umbrella grasses get tall, grow them in pots that are at least 1 gallon or larger so that they don't fall over. If the plant is not hardy in your area, bring it indoors during the colder months and set it in a tray of water.

Dwarf umbrella grasses add a graceful touch to a container.

CORKSCREW RUSH

Corkscrew rush (*Juncus effusus* 'Spiralis', Zones 6–9) has tightly coiled foliage whose upright form is perfect for containers. I like this rush because it is more interesting than those with straight foliage—and in a small container, you need plenty of interest. Since corkscrew rush doesn't like to have its crown submerged in the summer, position the plant so that its crown sits just above the water. Because it's a grass, it needs to be fed to stay green; otherwise, it will turn yellow and fail to grow. The foliage will kink if it gets manhandled, so if the dog likes to drink from your container, avoid this plant.

YELLOW MONKEY FLOWER

Yellow monkey flower (*Mimulus guttatus* and cvs., syn. *M. langsdorfii*, Zones 6–9) is a summer bloomer that likes a little shade. Reaching anywhere from 2 to 10 inches tall, it subtly weaves its way among other plants in the container, adding a touch of color. If you deadhead and feed this plant steadily throughout the summer, it will keep producing 1¹/₂-inch-long yellow flowers. It does best in shallow, moving water, especially when the water temperature rises above 65°F. If you don't have a pump, yellow monkey flower will still do fine.

Corkscrew rush has busy foliage to draw the eye.

PERFECT PLANTS

NAME	LIGHT	SIZE	WATER DEPTH
DWARF UMBRELLA GRASSES	Part sun to shade	2 to 4 feet tall and wide	Up to 4 inches above the crown
CORKSCREW RUSH	Sun to part shade	12 to 18 inches tall and wide	Just below the crown in summer or 2 inches above in cool weather
YELLOW MONKEY FLOWER	Part sun to shade	Up to 10 inches tall and wide	Up to the crown or 1 inch above in summer
WATER CLOVERS	Sun to shade	¼ inch to 6 inches tall with an indeterminate spread	Up to 4 inches above the crown
'CRUSHED ICE' ARROWHEAD	Sun to light shade	1 foot tall and wide	Up to 1 inch above the crown
DWARF PARROT FEATHER	Sun to shade	4 inches high with an indefinite spread	As deep as you can go without submerging the entire plant

'Crushed Ice' arrowhead has foliage that makes a splash.

'CRUSHED ICE' ARROWHEAD

The bold foliage and clean white flowers of arrowheads (*Sagittaria* spp. and cvs., Zones 5–11) make them great plants for water containers. Easy to grow in sun to light shade, they are rampant runners and can fill a container. Growing them in a 1-gallon pot will keep them in check and also make the plant look fuller. Arrowheads are heavy feeders. To keep them green, growing, and flowering in a small container, give them frequent doses of a fertilizer designed for water plants.

Arrowheads vary widely in height and leaf shape. I like 'Crushed Ice' arrowhead (*Sagittaria graminea* 'Crushed Ice') for a container because it is a great bloomer and gets only 1 foot tall and 1 foot wide. Best of all are the slender, variegated leaves, which are in proportion to a container but still provide visual interest. Where the summers get hot and humid, 'Crushed Ice' will benefit from afternoon shade.

WATER CLOVERS

The aptly named water clovers (*Marsilea* spp. and cvs., Zones 6–11) have attractive foliage that insinuates itself in and around the other plants in the container. As an added feature, the leaves close at night and resemble little butterflies sleeping on the water. These plants grow in sun or shade and are easy to care for, requiring only occasional feeding and thinning. Don't worry about overthinning— they don't mind a touch of ruthlessness when you cut them back. Many water clovers are hardy to Zone 6, but all are easy to grow indoors if need be. Because they grow from creeping rhizomes, any piece that has roots and a leaf will grow.

MOSQUITO SOLUTIONS

"West Nile virus," "spiral meningitis," and "mosquitoes"—combine these three terms and the result is an unwarranted fear of all bodies of water as a potential breeding ground for illness. The best habitat for mosquito larvae

Moving water equals no mosquitoes.

is actually shallow, stagnant water, which is not commonly found in backyard ponds. Mosquito larvae are air breathers, with a breathing tube like a snorkel that must break the surface of the water for them to take in air while they stay under water to look for food. If the water's surface is moving, it becomes virtually impossible for them to breathe, and they drown.

Products that control mosquito larvae are available to consumers. Items like mosquito pucks contain *Bacillus thuringiensis* spp. *israelensis*, which is a bacterium that will kill mosquito larvae (but has no effect on eggs or pupae). While they are effective, they must be replaced regularly.

There are more natural ways to keep mosquitoes at bay. A waterfall, a fountain, or an air bubbler keeps the surface water constantly moving, which will keep female mosquitoes from laying their eggs. Or you can install a small pump in container ponds, such as half barrels, to create a fountain or to swirl the

water gently, which will also discourage egg laying.

Fish are good at keeping out mosquitoes by eating them, but large fish, like koi, are often too big to feed on small larvae; guppies or killifish are more appropriate for this purpose. The trick is not to feed them—or, at least, feed them very little—because an outdoor pond has enough insects, algae, and other organisms to feed your fish naturally.

Plants can be useful in reducing the surface area of ponds. Waterlilies (*Nymphaea* cvs., USDA Hardiness Zones 3–11) are the best choice for this, but many floating plants will also block out mosquitoes. Be sure to check invasive reports (www.invasivespeciesinfo.gov/aquatics/main.shtml) before purchasing water plants, as many varieties are invasive.

—John Bueglas

Floating plants help block out mosquitoes.

Water clovers cover the feet of taller plants.

DWARF PARROT FEATHER

The common parrot feather (*Myriophyllum aquaticum*, Zones 6–11) is a mainstay of water gardens, and with good reason. Its soft, furry plumes are small but plentiful, and the fine texture makes an impact. Dwarf parrot feather (*Myriophyllum papillosum* var. *pulcherrima*, Zones 6–11) is a more refined relative of the common species and is perfect for water containers because it gets only half as tall (4 inches) as its ubiquitous cousin. Dwarf parrot feather needs only a 4-inch-diameter pot in which to grow, but it will spread over the surface of the water, hiding the pots of other plants and spilling over the edge of the container. Because it will float, dwarf parrot feather can be grown in deep water; just don't submerge it. This plant grows easily from stem cuttings. Simply take a bunch of it and add it to another pot in the container, or clip it to the side of the container. Overwintering cuttings in the house is just as easy.

Dwarf parrot feather carpets the water surface.

GREAT CONTAINER
GARDENS

Creating jaw-dropping container gardens is easy if you follow designer Todd Holloway's three basic principles—pick large containers, use many plants, and water and fertilize them well.

AS A PROFESSIONAL CONTAINER DESIGNER, I HAVE A FEW customers who want the biggest and best containers on the block. They like the attention, and they love to report that people stop to gawk and sometimes take pictures. So there is considerable pressure on me to push these containers over the top. Through the years, I've come up with a few strategies to do just that. With these basics under your belt, you'll be able to design your own big, bold, showstopping containers with dazzling combos of lush leaves and bewildering flowers.

1 Tropicanna® canna (*Canna indica* 'Phasion')

2 'Skyfire' coleus (*Solenostemon scutellarioides* 'Skyfire')

3 'Sweetheart Purple' sweet potato vine (*Ipomoea batatas* 'Sweetheart Purple')

4 'Goldsturm' black-eyed Susan (*Rudbeckia fulgida* var. *sullivantii* 'Goldsturm')

5 'Zwartkop' aeonium (*Aeonium* 'Zwartkop')

6 'Black Magic' elephant's ear (*Colocasia esculenta* 'Black Magic')

7 'Green on Green' plectranthus (*Plectranthus forsteri* 'Green on Green')

8 'Sweet Caroline Purple' sweet potato vine (*Ipomoea batatas* 'Sweet Caroline Purple')

9 Callie® Orange calibrachoa (*Calibrachoa* 'Callie Orange')

15 PERENNIALS THAT SHINE IN POTS

FOR SUN

Blue oat grass (*Helictotrichon sempervirens*, Zones 4–9)

Bowles' golden sedge (*Carex elata* 'Aurea', Zones 5–9)

Bronze fennel (*Foeniculum vulgare* 'Purpureum', Zones 4–9)

Lavenders (*Lavandula* spp. and cvs., Zones 5–10)

Michaelmas daisy (*Aster novi-belgii* 'Professor Anton Kippenberg', Zones 4–8)

Short fountain grasses (*Pennisetum alopecuroides* 'Moudry', 'Little Bunny', and 'Hameln', Zones 6–9)

Snow in summer (*Cerastium tomentosum* and cvs., Zones 3–7)

Spurges (*Euphorbia* spp. and cvs., Zones 4–11)

Wormwoods (*Artemisia* spp. and cvs., Zones 3–9)

FOR SHADE

American maidenhair fern (*Adiantum pedatum*, Zones 3–8)

Barrenworts (*Epimedium* spp. and cvs., Zones 4–9)

European wild ginger (*Asarum europaeum*, Zones 4–8)

Foam flowers (*Tiarella* spp. and cvs., Zones 3–9)

Lady's mantle (*Alchemilla mollis*, Zones 4–7)

Siberian buglosses (*Brunnera macrophylla* cvs., Zones 3–7)

—Christine Froelich

CHOOSE YOUR CONTAINER WISELY

A big, explosive display requires a large container. It must have enough volume to accommodate the roots of the plants' ultimate size. A stunning combination can be sustained within a smaller container, but it requires constant monitoring to ensure that the container is getting enough water, fertilizer, and pruning. Without the greenest of thumbs, a pot that's too small will almost always disappoint. At minimum, the container should accommodate a soil volume of at least half the size of the eventual volume of plants. This is important visually, as well.

I almost always use the rule of thirds when designing containers. The rule is based on an aesthetically pleasing compositional proportion used in painting, photography, and design. The rule can be used in one of two ways, each one opposite from the other. Starting with the container, visualize the overall look of the planting you desire according to your plants' eventual size. The container must take up either one-third or two-thirds of the eventual total height of the container and the plants together. And the plants must take up the remaining two-thirds or one-third, respectively, of the planting. If, for example, your pot is 2 feet tall, your plants' eventual height can either

1 Weeping yucca (*Yucca recurvifolia*)

2 'Hansel' rhododendron (*Rhododendron* 'Hansel')

3 'Ascot Rainbow' euphorbia (*Euphorbia × martinii* 'Ascot Rainbow')

4 Dwarf blue fescue (*Festuca glauca* cv.)

1. 'Morning Light' miscanthus (*Miscanthus sinensis* 'Morning Light')
2. 'Goldsturm' black-eyed Susan (*Rudbeckia fulgida* var. *sullivantii* 'Goldsturm')
3. 'Blackie' sweet potato vine (*Ipomoea batatas* 'Blackie')
4. Cigar flower (*Cuphea ignea*)
5. Golden creeping Jenny (*Lysimachia nummularia* 'Aurea')
6. Madness™ Red petunia (*Petunia* Madness™ Red)
7. Purple heart (*Tradescantia pallida* 'Purpurea')
8. 'Tilt A Whirl' coleus (*Solenostemon scutellarioides* 'Tilt A Whirl')

be 1 foot tall (which would have your planter being two-thirds of the overall height of 3 feet) or 4 feet tall (which would have your container being one-third of the overall height of 6 feet).

PILE IN THE PLANTS

I like to cram lots of different plants into one container for a lush, abundant look. I occasionally have to yank out some poor performers during the season, and it's nice to have lots of other favorites in the mix to keep the show going. But there is such a thing as too many plants. Rather than filling the entire surface of the soil with plants when potting up your container, leave a couple of inches between

each plant. This will give the plants a better chance of getting off to a good start. Adding new plants to a container later in the season doesn't seem to work for me. The soil surface is usually full of roots, which makes it difficult for new additions to establish themselves.

DON'T SKIMP ON THE WATER OR FERTILIZER

A pot stuffed with lots of plants requires lots of attention. Water is often the biggest issue later in the season, once the plants become larger and more mature. A container that fully dries out one or more times during the season can take weeks to recover and, in many cases, may never

HOW TO POT UP A LUSH CONTAINER

Follow these five easy steps and a gorgeous container is in your future.

1 Cover the drainage holes with a mesh screen to prevent them from clogging and to keep soil from washing through onto your patio or deck.

2 Fill the pot with soil up to a few inches from the top using a top-quality, all-purpose potting mix. This will leave room for the bulk of your plants' existing rootballs and soil. Add more soil if your plants are in small nursery pots.

3 Add slow-release fertilizer to the top of the soil. Using your fingers or a trowel, thoroughly and evenly work the fertilizer into the soil to a depth of 6 to 8 inches. Pack the soil and fertilizer mixture gently into the container with your hands, making sure there are no voids.

4 Plant large plants first, adding smaller plants as you move out toward the edges of the pot. Fill in with soil as you go, making sure not to cover the tops of the roots with more than half an inch of soil.

5 Water the container slowly, with your sprayer set to a gentle shower, for up to 10 minutes to allow the new soil to absorb the water properly. You can stop watering when the water is flowing freely out of the container's drainage holes.

reach its full potential. More important than the frequency of watering is how deeply you water. One way to ensure that you are watering thoroughly is to keep watering until water begins to drain freely out of the bottom of the container. If the soil in a container is extremely dry, however, water has a tendency to run off the surface of the soil and down the inside surface of the pot. In this case, water may be draining out of the pot, but the soil isn't truly getting wet, and you'll need to take special care to wet the soil thoroughly. Keep in mind that freshly planted containers use far less water than containers in the peak of summer. So adjust your watering habits to compensate for increased heat and plant sizes.

Achieving showstopping containers is impossible using water alone. Fertilizing is every bit as important as watering, especially in the limited root space of a container. Once the fertilizer has been used up, the roots have nowhere else to get it, unlike garden-dwelling plants.

The most foolproof method of fertilizing is to use a slow-release granular fertilizer. Make sure to read the instructions on the package to avoid using too much. If the plants need a boost during the season, you can apply an appropriate liquid fertilizer. It's often necessary to add a few applications of liquid fertilizer, especially in tightly planted containers. You only have the one season to get everything you can get out of your planters, so make it count!

1 'Dusky Chief' phormium
  (*Phormium* 'Dusky Chief')

2 Croton (*Codiaeum* cv.)

3 'Obsidian' heuchera
  (*Heuchera* 'Obsidian')

4 'Rage' chrysanthemum
  Chrysanthemum 'Rage')

5 Golden creeping Jenny
  (*Lysimachia nummularia* 'Aurea')

PLANTS FOR SMALL SPACES

SMALL GARDENS REQUIRE NOT JUST CREATIVE DESIGN BUT ALSO PLANTS that fit the space. Oftentimes typical varieties grow too big for use in smaller gardens, and you don't want to spend lots of time pruning to keep things in scale. That's where this section comes in. We have profiled dwarf varieties and typical varieties that stay small, even at full maturity. You will find a selection of edibles and ornamentals, of course, but you will also discover that you can grow trees and shrubs in your small garden, as well as grasses that won't grow too tall or spread over the whole garden. You're sure to find something for your pocket garden.

EDIBLES

'AMISH PASTE' TOMATO
Lycopersicon lycopersicum 'Amish Paste'

'Amish Paste' is an indeterminate but rather tame climber that is easily trellised or staked. It bears a huge, steady crop of large oval fruit, versatile enough for slicing or canning, meaty enough for paste, yet juicy enough for juicing. What also sets this heirloom apart is that it has consistently won taste tests here and in Australia. No matter what the weather, 'Amish Paste' has proven to be delicious and reliable.

—DAVID CAVAGNARO

'Amish Paste' tomato

'ARISTOTLE' BASIL
Ocimum basilicum 'Aristotle'

Affectionately called "basketball basil," 'Aristotle' is an ultra-compact Greek variety. It has a neat, rounded habit that requires no pruning to maintain its shape. The form may be unique, but 'Aristotle' still maintains a pungent, classic flavor. The plants grow to be 12 to 14 inches tall and wide, making them perfect for container pots or small vegetable gardens.

—DANIELLE SHERRY

'Aristotle' basil

'ATLANTIS' BROCCOLI
Brassica oleracea 'Atlantis'

A high-yield miniature broccoli, 'Atlantis' is similar in taste and tenderness to the popular supermarket broccolini (the florets on top taste like broccoli, but the stems are tender and sweet like asparagus). Cut the main floret as soon as it matures to encourage additional side-shoot production. If harvested one to two times per week, the plants will bear small but sweet florets for four to six weeks depending on your zone.

—*FINE GARDENING* EDITORS

'BUSH PICKLE' CUCUMBER
Cucumis sativus 'Bush Pickle'

'Bush Pickle' has short, contained vines, so it won't engulf your entire pot. Expect a large harvest of sweet mini cukes.

—DANIELLE SHERRY

'Bush Pickle' cucumber

'FEHEROZON' PEPPER
Solanaceae capsicum 'Feherozon'

'Feherozon' is a pointed, pimento-type Hungarian pepper that starts out yellow and turns orange-red when ripe. The small plants are often so loaded with big peppers that one can hardly see the leaves.

—DAVID CAVAGNARO

'Feherozon' pepper

'GREEN SAUSAGE' TOMATO
Lycopersicon lycopersicum 'Green Sausage'

This compact plant is perfect to grow in hanging baskets. The green-and-amber-striped plum tomatoes have firm flesh with a rich, sweet flavor, making this a great sauce tomato.

—DANIELLE SHERRY

'IVORY' EGGPLANT
Solanum melongena 'Ivory'

Those who love white eggplant because of its mild, smooth taste will be thrilled to grow the variety 'Ivory' because of its dense habit and high yield. The fruit is roughly the size of a baseball—perfect for cooking. If space is a consideration, this plant would do well in containers.

—DANIELLE SHERRY

LEMON THYME
Thymus × citriodorus **and cvs.**
ZONES: 6–9

Lemon thyme, known for its intense lemon aroma, is at its best in tight spaces. It can be a scraggly mat in the ground; confined in a container, however, it's an attractive, upright mound of small, pointed, glossy green leaves. As the branches grow, they spread out and trail over the container's edge; by early summer, they produce dense heads of lilac flowers that last well over a month.

—JO ANN GARDNER

Lemon thyme

'RAMBLING RED STRIPE' TOMATO
Lycopersicon lycopersicum 'Rambling Red Stripe'

This variety has a compact growth habit, making it perfect for a cramped hanging basket. The foliage is fernlike in appearance and extremely fuzzy, while the sweet-tasting red-and-green-striped fruit hang in clustered bunches at the tips of the branches.

—DANIELLE SHERRY

'Rambling Red Stripe' tomato

'SAFFRON' SUMMER SQUASH
Cucurbita pepo 'Saffron'

'Saffron' summer squash has the creamiest, most delicious flesh you'll ever taste. Compact plants produce prolifically and are extremely sturdy.

—DANIELLE SHERRY

'Saffron' summer squash

SALAD BURNET
Sanguisorba minor
ZONES: 4–8

This is one of the earliest and hardiest culinary herbs out there. The plant is not very big, stretching only to a foot tall when in flower. Its tiny ruffled foliage has a delicate cucumber scent and flavor. Salad burnet is neat and tidy, making it perfect to place at the edge of a garden. Its unique geometric flowers are the icing on the cake.

—ANNE DUNCAN

Salad burnet

'SUNSHINE BLUE' HIGHBRUSH BLUEBERRY
Vaccinium 'Sunshine Blue'

Should you be short on space, this neatly mounded variety grows well on a sunny patio in a 24- to 36-inch-diameter pot. 'Sunshine Blue' highbush blueberry is self-pollinating, so you only need one to get berries—but you may find it's hard to resist buying another.

—STEPHANIE TURNER

'Sunshine Blue' highbush blueberry

'SWEET 'N' NEAT CHERRY RED' TOMATO
Lycopersicon esculentum 'Sweet 'n' Neat Cherry Red'

This dwarf, determinate tomato will produce high yields of small, delicious-tasting fruit. 'Sweet 'n' Neat Cherry Red' is the perfect tomato for growing in containers. The entire plant will only reach about 14 inches tall, so it will need some staking to support the heavy fruit load.

—DANIELLE SHERRY

ORNAMENTALS

'BLUE MOUSE EARS' HOSTA
Hosta 'Blue Mouse Ears'
ZONES: 3–8

Petite, rubbery leaves in a soft shade of blue make the award-winning 'Blue Mouse Ears' easy to love. Low growing and perfectly symmetrical, this adorable miniature hosta blooms profusely in midsummer, sending up stems that peak at just 1 foot tall. It's also slug resistant.

—JOHN O'BRIEN

'Blue Mouse Ears' Hosta

DWARF IRISES
Iris reticulata and cvs.
ZONES: 5–8

Individually, dwarf irises may get lost, but when planted in clusters of a dozen or more bulbs, like 'Harmony' (pictured), these colorful, outsize blossoms are dazzling in the early-spring garden. Their sweet fragrance lures early-flying pollinators. Plant a variety of dwarf irises for a long blooming season.

—SUSAN J. TWELT

'Harmony' dwarf irises

'FANCY WHEELER' BLANKET FLOWER
Gaillardia aristata 'Fancy Wheeler'
ZONES: 3–9

'Fancy Wheeler' is a true dwarf cultivar, only reaching about a foot tall and wide. Its compact growth habit doesn't stop, however, with the foliage. In late spring, the plant is completely covered with buds that will open right at the edge of the leaves, creating a little tidy cushion of color that is more in line with an annual bedding plant than a leggy perennial. These blooms, with their deep red center and lemon yellow edge, cover the plants throughout the summer.

—JEREMY WEBBER

'HUMMINGBIRD' SUMMERSWEET
Clethra alnifolia 'Hummingbird'
ZONES: 3–9

Summersweet is aptly named, being a shrub with fragrant, fluffy bottlebrush-type flowers, which display their charms during July and August, attracting butterflies and bees. This mounding cultivar produces good bloom in shady or sunny locations, a unique trait among summer-flowering shrubs. Once the summer blooms fade, its fall leaves turn a pleasing yellow.

—BOBBIE SCHWARTZ

'JAMES COMPTON' BUGBANE
Actaea simplex 'James Compton'
ZONES: 4–8

The bronzy foliage of 'James Compton' serves as a springboard for its dark, wiry, branched stems and a plethora of pinkish white flowers that open from purple buds.

'Hummingbird' Summersweet

Not blooming until late September or early October, 'James Compton' will spice up the fall shade garden.

—BOBBIE SCHWARTZ

LITTLE TRUDY™ CATMINT
Nepeta Little Trudy™
ZONES: 4–9

This hybrid, with the cultivar name 'Psfike', only reaches 8 to 10 inches tall and 12 to 16 inches wide, the perfect size for containers, bed edges, or other small nooks and crannies. It features the same silvery foliage and summer lavender blooms that we know and love, and it thrives in full sun to partial shade and well-drained soil.

—*FINE GARDENING* EDITORS

Little Trudy catmint

'MERINGUE' PURPLE CONEFLOWER
Echinacea purpurea 'Meringue'

Gardeners go gaga for 'Meringue' because it looks so different. This is a short coneflower with creamy, light yellow-green flowers. The top looks like a pom-pom surrounded by single petals at the base. This plant is exceptionally sturdy. Although the blossoms are smaller than other double-flowered cultivars, there are tons of them and they cover the plant throughout most of the summer.

–STEPHANIE COHEN

'Meringue' purple coneflower

OSO EASY® SERIES ROSES
Rosa Oso Easy® series cvs.
ZONES: 4–9

These roses are blooming machines with glossy green foliage, which, thankfully, seems to be neglected by Japanese beetles. The delectable names are quite apt: 'Cherry Pie' (pictured), for example, is a yummy cherry red with a white eye and yellow stamens, while 'Paprika' is an orange-and-yellow bicolor that fades to a lovely pale apricot with melon edges.

–BOBBIE SCHWARTZ

Oso Easy series roses

'SEM' FALSE SPIREA
Sorbaria sorbifolia 'Sem'
ZONES: 2–8

Denser than the species, 'Sem' has pinkish red foliage, which unfurls in spring on deep pink stems, the color gradually changing to harmonious shades of soft lime and chartreuse accented with tints of bronze-red on the young tips. In midsummer, the textured leaves turn completely green, and then, in autumn, 'Sem' produces another burst of color that varies from yellow to orange to rust.

–BOBBIE SCHWARTZ

'Sem' false spirea

SIAM TULIP
Curcuma alismatifolia
ZONES: 8–11

This ginger has it all: It is a well-mannered, eye-catching plant that sports a long-lasting bloom in the garden or as a cut flower. It is also free of diseases and insects. Siam tulip is available in yellow, white, and many shades of pink, and it may also be used as a container plant.

–MARION DRUMMOND

Siam tulip

ZEBRA HAWORTHIA
Haworthia attenuata
ZONE: 11

Rub your finger along the leaves of this crocodile of a succulent to feel the unique hard warts that pock the surface. Though small, zebra hawor-thia's hard, leathery surface makes it downright hard to kill—except with excess water or frost. This plant is a favorite for shallow bowls or bonsai pots, where it offsets freely, soon filling up the pot. It blooms on long piano-wire stalks with small, simple white flowers.

–MAUREEN GILMER

Zebra haworthia

GRASSES

'THE BLUES' LITTLE BLUESTEM
Schizachyrium scoparium 'The Blues'
ZONES: 2–7

Little bluestem typically ranges in color from shades of blue to green, but 'The Blues' features the color of the prairie sky, holding true through summer. The entire plant turns shades of orange, red, and purple in fall. Adaptable to harsh conditions, it tolerates even alkaline and saline soils. The extensive root system makes it impervious to drought, so hold the water and give it plenty of sunshine (at least six hours).

–SCOTT VOGT

'GOLD BAR' DWARF VARIEGATED MISCANTHUS
Miscanthus sinensis 'Gold Bar'
ZONES: 5–9

Similar to zebra grass, 'Gold Bar' is a showstopper, with its dense and dramatic horizontal gold-colored striping. It is exceptionally upright and compact in habit. At the end of October, burgundy inflorescences appear just about the blades. Its late bloom means that it will not have time to seed.

–BOBBIE SCHWARTZ

GOLDEN DWARF SWEET FLAG
Acorus gramineus 'Ogon'
ZONES: 6–9

This tidy sweet flag has a consistent look all season. Its fan-shaped form helps direct the eye into or out of a container design, while its slow-growing nature provides a consistent ray of gold at the base of a container without taking over the combo. Golden dwarf sweet flag is also frost tolerant, adding extra weeks of visual impact in spring and fall.

–*FINE GARDENING* EDITORS

Golden dwarf sweet flag

PRAIRIE DROPSEED
Sporobolus heterolepis
ZONES: 3–8

In August and September, wispy, fragrant flower spikes over narrow, deep green leaves make prairie dropseed a standout in any setting. It is graceful in all seasons of the year, including autumn, when hues of golden orange develop. This grass grows best in dry to evenly moist soil.

–SCOTT VOGT

Prairie dropseed

PURPLE LOVEGRASS
Eragrostis spectabilis
ZONES: 5–9

As summer ends, the fluffy, reddish bronze flowers of purple lovegrass develop and cover the entire plant, while the bright green foliage turns shades of red and orange. This plant is tolerant of a wide range of soils, even infertile sand. For tight soil, just raise the bed a few inches to allow the soil to drain after a rain. This short-lived grass grows for three to five years but may grow longer if uncrowded. Given plenty of sun, it will be happy wherever it is planted.

–SCOTT VOGT

Purple lovegrass

RIVER OATS
Chasmanthium latifolium
ZONES: 5–9

River oats is one of the most adaptable and ornamental native grasses. It thrives in sun or shade, while the flat, oatlike seed heads add interest, giving the plant its nickname: "fish on a line." These lime green seed heads elongate and turn light tan in winter, as the broad leaves and upright habit of the plant complement them. In the wild, it grows in moist soil in wooded areas and along streams, so plants in full sun will need supplemental irrigation through periods of drought.

–SCOTT VOGT

TREES & SHRUBS

'ANNE MARIE' LANTANA
Lantana camara 'Anne Marie'
ZONES: 8–11

Most relatives of 'Anne Marie' become large, sprawling shrubs, but this compact shrub stays below 2 feet tall. It blooms profusely from spring through summer featuring confetti-colored flowers with a yellow center radiating out to pink. 'Anne Marie' is salt and drought tolerant and is an excellent butterfly attractor.

—BOB COOK

'Anne Marie' lantana

'CAVATINE' JAPANESE PIERIS
Pieris japonica 'Cavatine'
ZONES: 5–9

This little shrub packs a serious punch. Its dense, dark green foliage forms a tight, compact mound. In early spring, 'Cavatine' is covered in bell-like white flowers, making the shrub look like a fluffy white snowball. Because it stays small, this Japanese pieris is sometimes mistaken for a unique new perennial. Best of all, deer avoid it.

—DANIELLE SHERRY

'Cavatine' Japanese pieris

DWARF BLUE SPRUCE
Picea pungens 'Globosa'
ZONES: 2–8

This diminutive evergreen (perhaps more aptly called "everblue") will chase away the blues through the cold winter months.

—*FINE GARDENING* EDITORS

Dwarf blue spruce

DWARF PALMETTO
Sabal minor
ZONES: 7–10

Palms generally need good drainage, but the dwarf palmetto is right at home in swampy areas. A trunkless species, the growing point stays near ground level while the fronds grow up in a fountainlike arrangement. The fan-shaped fronds provide wonderful texture. This plant is smaller in dry locations.

—DAN GILL

'FIREFLY' HEATHER
Calluna vulgaris 'Firefly'
ZONES: 4–7

This is not your typical evergreen because it's usually not green at all. The scaly foliage of 'Firefly' is a unique terra-cotta color for most of the year and turns a brilliant brick red in cool temperatures (see photo); soft mauve flowers appear in fall. The best attribute of heathers is their ability to thrive in the tough-

est of conditions (they originated on the European moorlands, where strong winds and poor soil prevail). Lean, sharply drained soils are not a problem, so 'Firefly' is an ideal roadside plant.

—DANIELLE SHERRY

'Firefly' heather

LAVENDER TWIST™ EASTERN REDBUD
Cercis canadensis 'Covey'
ZONES: 5–9

Lavender Twist is a small weeping cultivar, noted for its absence of an upright leader and for its dense umbrella-shaped crown with contorted stems and pendulous branches. Its gray bark and unique shape are two of its best features, particularly noticeable during the winter when it is leafless. The height is manageable, varying from 5 to 10 feet, depending on whether it has been staked and trained.

—BOBBIE SCHWARTZ

LITTLE GIRL SERIES MAGNOLIA
Magnolia Little Girl series cvs.
ZONES: 5–9

Those with small spaces might want to avail themselves of one of the Little Girl series of magnolias, most of which top out at 10 feet (although they can grow to 15 feet under optimal conditions). There are eight cultivars in the Little Girl series, varying in color from reddish purple to pink. The two most common in production are 'Ann' (pictured) and 'Betty'. Their floral display occurs approximately two weeks later than the species, decreasing the possibility of spring frost damage, which turns the blossoms to mush.

—BOBBIE SCHWARTZ

Little Girl series magnolia

LITTLE HENRY® VIRGINIA SWEETSPIRE
Itea virginica 'Sprich'
ZONES: 6–9

Virginia sweetspire is a deciduous shrub native to the southeastern United States, so it's well suited to moist low-lying areas. Little Henry is a compact selection of 'Henry's Garnet', a popular cultivar known for its attractive flower clusters and rich burgundy fall color. This small shrub shines in spring, when numerous upright and drooping racemes of small white flowers appear, and again in autumn, when the brilliant fall color puts on a show.

—DAN GILL

Little Henry Virginia sweetspire

'LITTLE JOHN' DWARF CALLISTEMON
Callistemon viminalis 'Little John'
ZONES: 9–11

The rosy red bottlebrush flowers of 'Little John' are stunning against the blue-green foliage. The plant blooms profusely in summer but will also blossom sporadically throughout the year. The low-growing shrub is evergreen, too, making it a perfect candidate for foundation plantings. Hummingbirds will actually battle each other to get near it, but deer will leave it alone.

—MICHELLE GERVAIS

MEYER LILAC
Syringa meyeri
ZONES: 4–7

Most classic lilacs grow quite tall and leggy without annual pruning; fortunately, Meyer lilac will stay much smaller. Although the catalogs promise growth of 4 to 6 feet, it will try to stretch a bit more. Some judicious pruning every two or three years, just after bloom, will keep it to the desired size. The dark green leaves are small. In fall, they turn a vibrant burgundy red.

—BOBBIE SCHWARTZ

Meyer lilac

'RUBY SLIPPERS' OAKLEAF HYDRANGEA
Hydrangea quercifolia 'Ruby Slippers'
ZONES: 5–9

'Ruby Slippers', a new compact form of oakleaf hydrangea, is a must-have for smaller spaces. 'Ruby Slippers' boasts a multitude of stocky flowers that show up as white and then mature to striking deep rose. With its space-conscious habit and vibrant blooms, 'Ruby Slippers' will soon become a hugely popular flowering shrub.

—ANDY PULTE

'Ruby Slippers' oakleaf hydrangea

'SLENDER SILHOUETTE' SWEETGUM
Liquidambar styraciflua 'Slender Silhouette'
ZONES: 5–10

'Slender Silhouette' is a compact, columnar tree with an impressive mature height and a width of only 3 to 6 feet, so it takes up little precious space. Its great architectural form makes it a focal point like no other. Unlike other sweetgums, which drop scores of macelike fruit all over the place, 'Slender Silhouette' produces minimal fruit, which drop in a small area due to the tree's narrow structure. This sweetgum's foliage is deep green in summer and then turns yellow, orange, red, or burgundy in fall. It also tolerates a wide range of soils, including clay.

—MARY ANNE THORNTON

'SOMERSET' DAPHNE
Daphne × burkwoodii 'Somerset'
ZONES: 5–8

If anyone were to claim to love daphnes for any reason other than their wonderfully fragrant flowers, then he or she would be lying. The smell is somewhere between a root-beer soda and baby powder, putting a smile on the face of anyone lucky enough to sniff them. An added bonus is their compact evergreen foliage (in cool zones, plants may only be semievergreen). Some daphnes have a bad reputation for being finicky, but 'Somerset' is one of the hardiest cultivars.

–DANIELLE SHERRY

'Somerset' daphne

'TOM THUMB' COTONEASTER
Cotoneaster 'Tom Thumb'
ZONES: 5–7

This tidy, virtuous cotoneaster grows low to the ground and is self-rooting, making it a useful underplanting or ground cover. Unlike most cotoneasters, it doesn't gobble up space. Instead, the aptly named 'Tom Thumb' remains compact at 8 to 12 inches tall with an eventual spread of 3 to 6 feet. It requires little or no pruning. This miniature deciduous shrub doesn't flower or fruit, but its leaves turn a brilliant red in the fall.

–CHRISTINE FROELICH

'Tom Thumb' cotoneaster

'TWOMBLY RED SENTINEL' JAPANESE MAPLE
Acer palmatum 'Twombly Red Sentinel'
ZONES: 5–8

This Japanese maple is a slow-growing, upright variety with a compact form that features deep burgundy leaves. The foliage turns a striking red in fall and remains on the tree for an extended period, usually until Thanksgiving. This tree combines nicely with conifers in a mixed border or rock garden, and it works well near a patio or house entry. Like other maples, 'Twombly Red Sentinel' belongs in full sun or partial shade and in fertile, well-drained soil.

–_FINE GARDENING_ EDITORS

'Twombly Red Sentinel' Japanese maple

'WISSEL'S SAGUARO' FALSE CYPRESS
Chamaecyparis lawsoniana 'Wissel's Saguaro'
ZONES: 5–8

The sculptural habit of this conifer is invaluable for tight spaces because it ultimately gets only 2 feet wide. Best of all, the design possibilities of 'Wissel's Saguaro' false cypress are endless. It can be an excellent vertical focal point in the midst of a bed, it can anchor the corner of a building, or it can add height to a narrow side garden. Younger plants are also perfect for planting in containers. In spring, the new growth is a bit brighter, adding soft highlights to each branch.

–KAREN CHAPMAN

'Wissel's Saguaro' false cypress

USDA HARDINESS ZONE MAP

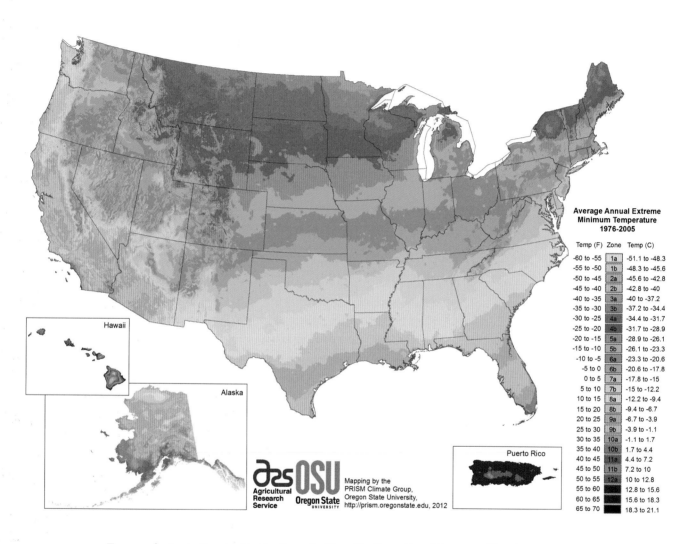

Average Annual Extreme Minimum Temperature 1976-2005		
Temp (F)	Zone	Temp (C)
-60 to -55	1a	-51.1 to -48.3
-55 to -50	1b	-48.3 to -45.6
-50 to -45	2a	-45.6 to -42.8
-45 to -40	2b	-42.8 to -40
-40 to -35	3a	-40 to -37.2
-35 to -30	3b	-37.2 to -34.4
-30 to -25	4a	-34.4 to -31.7
-25 to -20	4b	-31.7 to -28.9
-20 to -15	5a	-28.9 to -26.1
-15 to -10	5b	-26.1 to -23.3
-10 to -5	6a	-23.3 to -20.6
-5 to 0	6b	-20.6 to -17.8
0 to 5	7a	-17.8 to -15
5 to 10	7b	-15 to -12.2
10 to 15	8a	-12.2 to -9.4
15 to 20	8b	-9.4 to -6.7
20 to 25	9a	-6.7 to -3.9
25 to 30	9b	-3.9 to -1.1
30 to 35	10a	-1.1 to 1.7
35 to 40	10b	1.7 to 4.4
40 to 45	11a	4.4 to 7.2
45 to 50	11b	7.2 to 10
50 to 55	12a	10 to 12.8
55 to 60		12.8 to 15.6
60 to 65		15.6 to 18.3
65 to 70		18.3 to 21.1

Mapping by the
PRISM Climate Group,
Oregon State University,
http://prism.oregonstate.edu, 2012

Those gardening in Canada should refer to the Plant Hardiness Zone Map created by the Canadian Forest Service, which can be found online at http://planthardiness.gc.ca.

SOURCES

Ornamentals

Big Dipper Farm
Black Diamond, Washington
360-886-8253
www.bigdipperfarm.com

Fieldstone Gardens
Vassalboro, Maine
207-923-3836
www.fieldstonegardens.com

Forestfarm
Williams, Oregon
541-846-7269
www.forestfarm.com

Edibles

The Chile Woman
Bloomington, Indiana
812-339-8321
www.thechilewoman.com

Cross Country Nurseries
Rosemont, New Jersey
908-996-4646
www.chileplants.com

Johnny's Selected Seeds
Waterville, Maine
877-564-6697
www.johnnyseeds.com

Jung Seeds & Plants
Randolph, Wisconsin
800-297-3123
www.jungseed.com

The Pepper Gal
Fort Lauderdale, Florida
954-537-5540
www.peppergal.com

Stokes Seeds
Buffalo, New York
800-396-9238
www.stokeseeds.com

CONTRIBUTORS

Jeffrey Bale's garden design business is based in Portland, Oregon.

Jennifer Bartley tends her kitchen garden in Granville, Ohio, and is the author of *Designing the New Kitchen Garden*.

Jennifer Benner is a horticulturist and former *Fine Gardening* associate editor in Roxbury, Connecticut.

Daryl Beyers is a former assistant editor at *Fine Gardening*.

Pamela Bird gardens in Fairfax, California, where she grows produce for 10 families on a quarter acre.

Steve Biskey and **Mark Watters** garden in the Catskill Mountains, near Parksville, New York.

John Bueglas is an entomologist and operator of Dubé Botanical Gardens in Antigonish, Nova Scotia.

Sarah Bush is the owner of Edible Revolution, a kitchen-garden design and installation firm in Knoxville, Tennessee.

David Cavagnaro has trialed over 15,000 heirloom vegetables for Seed Savers Exchange in Decorah, Iowa.

Karen Chapman is a garden designer in Duvall, Washington.

Linda Chisari is a landscape designer in Southern California, where she gardens year-round.

Ron Clancy gardens in Vancouver, British Columbia, and has been growing peas since the 1960s.

Stephanie Cohen is known across the garden world as the "Perennial Diva." Each year she trials new plants in her Pennsylvania garden.

Bob Cook is a certified horticultural professional who gardens and teaches in Fort Myers, Florida.

William Cullina is the author of *Native Trees, Shrubs, and Vines* and cultivates his passion for plants in coastal Maine.

Darcy Daniels, of Bloomtown Gardens, designs residential gardens in Portland, Oregon.

Keith Davitt is a landscape designer, landscape contractor, and horticulturist. He has spent the last 20 years designing and building landscape projects around the country.

Glenn Drowns grows and saves seed from 700 varieties of squash in Calamus, Iowa.

Marion Drummond is executive director of the Mobile Botanical Gardens in Mobile, Alabama.

Anne Duncan and her husband own the Salem Herbfarm in Salem, Connecticut.

Scott Endres is co-owner of Tangletown Gardens, a retail garden center and landscape-design firm in Minneapolis, Minnesota. He gardens in St. Paul.

Christine Froehlich is a garden designer in Sodus Point, New York.

Jo Ann Gardner is coauthor, along with her husband, Jigs, of *Gardens of Use and Delight*. She writes from her home in Westport, New York.

Jim Garner is associate professor of horticulture at Horry-Georgetown Technical College in Myrtle Beach, South Carolina.

Peter Garnham is a master gardener and commercial grower of culinary herbs and speciality vegetables in East Hampton, New York.

Michelle Gervais is a senior editor for *Fine Gardening*.

Dan Gill is a consumer horticulturist at the Louisiana State University Agricultural Center in Baton Rouge.

Jeff Gillman, author of *The Truth About Organic Gardening*, is an associate professor of horticulture at the University of Minnesota in St. Paul.

Maureen Gilmer, horticulturist and author of *Palm Springs–Style Gardening*, resides in Morongo Valley, California.

Amy Goldman gardens in upstate New York and is the author of *Melons for the Passionate Grower*.

Billy Goodnick is a contributing editor to *Fine Gardening* and a landscape architect and educator in Santa Barbara, California.

Sandra Gorry is a horticulturist and garden designer who lives in New York City.

Jennie Hammill is a passionate gardener, piano teacher, and accomplished woodworker in Seattle, Washington.

Cynthia Hizer is an avid vegetable gardener in Covington, Georgia.

Todd Holloway is a container designer in Vancouver, British Columbia, and owner of Pot, Inc.

Lucinda Hutson is the author of *The Herb Garden Cookbook*. She lives, gardens, and entertains in Austin, Texas.

Reita Jackson is a writer and co-owner of a bed-and-breakfast in Starkville, Mississippi.

T.A. Johnson installs drip irrigation systems around Salt Lake City, Utah.

Tom Johnson is the director of gardens at Magnolia Plantation and Garden in Charleston, South Carolina.

Janet Macunovich owns a landscape design firm in Waterford, Michigan, and is the author of *Caring for Perennials* and *Easy Garden Design*.

Mary Ann McGourty is a garden designer and lecturer in northwest Connecticut.

Patti Moreno is an urban, organic vegetable gardener in Roxbury, Massachusetts.

Susan Morrison owns Creative Exteriors Landscape Design in Concord, California.

Melinda Myers teaches horticulture in Milwaukee and hosts radio and television shows on gardening.

John O'Brien is the owner of O'Brien Nurserymen, which sells more than 1,100 hosta varieties, in Granby, Connecticut.

Nancy J. Ondra, author of *The Perennial Care Manual*, tends her garden in Bucks County, Pennsylvania.

Fred Pappalardo gardens and creates compost with ease in Provincetown, Massachusetts.

Judith Phillips is the author of four books about gardening in the Southwest. She lives in Veguita, New Mexico.

Andy Pulte is on the faculty of the Department of Plant Sciences at the University of Tennessee in Knoxville.

Erin Ray is a garden designer in Portland, Oregon.

Rebecca Sams and her partner, Buell Steelman, own Mosaic Gardens, a landscape design/build company in Eugene, Oregon.

Bobbie Schwartz, a fellow of the Association of Professional Landscape Designers, is the owner of Bobbie's Green Thumb in Shaker Heights, Ohio.

Danielle Sherry is Senior Editor for *Fine Gardening*.

Megan F. Smith lives and tends her garden in Seattle, Washington.

Greg Speichert, coauthor of *Encyclopedia of Water Garden Plants*, lives in northwest Indiana.

Sylvia Thompson is the author of *The Kitchen Garden*.

Mary Anne Thornton gardens in Louisville, Kentucky, and serves on the boards of the Yew Dell Botanical Gardens, the Olmsted Parks Conservancy, and the Bernheim Arboretum.

Stephanie Turner is president of the National Garden Bureau and a horticulturist in Greenwood, South Carolina.

Susan J. Twelt, author of *The Rocky Mountain Garden Survival Guide*, gardens from her home in Salida, Colorado.

Scott Vogt is a horticulturist and grounds manager at Dyck Arboretum of the Plants in Hesston, Kansas.

Jeremy Webber is the director of field operations for Sunny Border Nurseries in Kensington, Connecticut.

CREDITS

All photos and illustrations are courtesy of *Fine Gardening* magazine © The Taunton Press, Inc., except as noted below:

vi: Photo by Brandi Spade

p. 4: Photo by Virginia Small

p. 6: Illustration by Allison Starcher

p. 8: Photos by Jennifer Benner

p. 9: Photos by Virginia Small

p. 12: Photo by Scott Phillips

pp. 14–15: Photos by Steve Aitken

P. 17: Photos by Scott Phillips (top left); Steve Aitken (bottom left); Jennifer Benner (right)

p. 19: Illustration © Chuck Lockhart

p. 20: Photo by Scott Phillips

pp. 22–23: Photos by Scott Phillips

p. 24: Illustration by Michael Gellatly

p. 25: Photo by John Bray, courtesy of *Kitchen Garden* magazine © The Taunton Press, Inc.

p. 26: Photo by Jennifer Benner

p. 28: Photo by Brent Benner

p. 30: Photo by Jennifer Benner

p. 31: Photo by Brent Benner

p. 32: Photos by Kathy Martin

p. 34: Illustrations by Louise M. Smith

p. 35: Photo by Boyd Hagen, courtesy *Kitchen Garden* magazine © The Taunton Press, Inc.

p. 36: Photo by Ruth Lively, courtesy *Kitchen Garden* magazine © The Taunton Press, Inc.

p. 37: Photo by Kathy Martin

p. 38: Photos © Kerry Ann Moore (top left); Danielle Sherry (top right and bottom right); Scott Phillips (bottom left)

p. 41: Photos © Kerry Ann Moore (top left); Stephanie Fagan (top right); Boyd Hagen, courtesy *Kitchen Garden* magazine © The Taunton Press, Inc. (bottom left); Danielle Sherry (bottom right)

p. 43: Illustrations by Dolores R. Santoliquido

p. 44: Photo © Derek St. Romaine

p. 46: Photo by Melissa Lucas

pp. 48-49: Photos by Melissa Lucas

p. 50: Photos by Marc Vassallo, courtesy *Kitchen Garden* magazine © The Taunton Press, Inc. (top far left and top center left); Jennifer Brown (center far left); © Derek St. Romaine (center left, bottom center left, and bottom right); Michelle Gervais (bottom left); © Andre Baranowski (top center right); Jennifer Benner (top far right); © Reita Jackson (bottom center right)

p. 51: Photo © Nancy J. Ondra

p. 52: Photo by Melissa Lucas

p. 53: Photo © Nancy J. Ondra

p. 54: Photo © Darcy Daniels

pp. 56-58: Photos © Darcy Daniels

p. 59: Photo © Jennifer Bartley

p. 60: Photo by Danielle Sherry

p. 62: Photo by Danielle Sherry

p. 63: Illustration by Martha Garstang Hill

pp. 64–65: Photos by Danielle Sherry

pp. 66–71: Photos by staff, courtesy *Kitchen Garden* magazine © The Taunton Press, Inc.

p. 72: Photo by Stephanie Fagan

p. 74: Photos by Rosalind Wanke, courtesy *Kitchen Garden* magazine © The Taunton Press, Inc.

p. 75: Illustration by Gary Williamson, courtesy *Kitchen Garden* magazine © The Taunton Press, Inc.

p. 76: Photo by Rosalind Wanke, courtesy *Kitchen Garden* magazine © The Taunton Press, Inc.

p. 77: Photo by Scott Phillips, courtesy *Kitchen Garden* magazine © The Taunton Press, Inc.

pp. 78-79: Photos by Scott Phillips

p. 79: Illustrations Wendy Bowes

p. 80: Photo by Jennifer Brown

pp. 82-83: Photos by Jennifer Brown

p. 84: Photo © Adam Gibbs

p. 86: Photo © Adam Gibbs

p. 87: Photo by Steven Cominsky

pp. 88-89: Photos © Adam Gibbs (top left, center left, top right, bottom left, bottom right); Danielle Sherry (bottom center)

p. 90: Photo by Scott Phillips, courtesy *Fine Cooking* magazine © The Taunton Press, Inc.

p. 92: Photo by Danielle Sherry

p. 94: Photos by John Bray, courtesy *Kitchen Garden* magazine © The Taunton Press, Inc. (left); Scott Phillips, courtesy *Fine Cooking* magazine © The Taunton Press, Inc. (right)

p. 95: Photos by Bernhard Michaelis/www.dreamstime.com (top left); courtesy of Johnny's Selected Seeds (top right and bottom)

p. 96: Photo by Scott Phillips

p. 98: Photo by Marc Vassallo, courtesy *Kitchen Garden* magazine © The Taunton Press, Inc.

p. 99–100: Photos © David Cavagnaro

p. 100: Illustration by Chuck Lockhart

p. 101: Photo by Danielle Sherry

p. 102: Photo by Steve Silk

p. 104: Photo © Ann E. Stratton

p. 106: Photos by courtesy Ted Dobson (top); © Buell Steelman (bottom)

pp. 107–108: Illustrations by Beverley Colgan

p. 109: Photos © Buell Steelman

p. 110: Photos by Danielle Sherry

p. 112: Illustration by Martha Garstang Hill

pp. 112-115: Photos by Danielle Sherry

p. 116: Photo © Allan Mandell

pp. 118-120: Photos © Allan Mandell

p. 121: Photo courtesy Jeffrey Bale

p. 122: Illustrations by Melissa Buntin

p. 123: Photos by courtesy Jeffrey Bale (top); © Allan Mandell

pp. 124–127: Photos © Allan Mandell

pp. 128–129: Illustration by Beverley Colgan

p. 130: Photo by Steve Aitken

pp. 132–133: Photos by Steve Aitken

p. 134: Photo by Steve Silk

pp. 136–138: Photos by Steve Silk; illustrations by Vincent Babak

p. 139: Illustration by Vincent Babak; photos by Jennifer Benner (top); Michelle Gervais (bottom)

p. 140: Photo by Jennifer Brown

p. 142: Illustration by Melissa Buntin

pp. 143–144: Photos by Jennifer Brown

p. 145: Illustration by Melissa Buntin

pp. 146–147: Photos by Jennifer Brown

p. 148: Photo by Brandi Spade

p. 150: Illustration by Grace McEnaney

p. 151: Photo by Brandi Spade

p. 152: Photos by Brandi Spade (bottom); courtesy Erin Ray (top)

p. 153: Photos by Brandi Spade (top); courtesy Erin Ray (bottom)

pp. 154–155: Photos by Brandi Spade

p. 156–159: Photos and illustrations by Michelle Gervais

pp. 160–161: Photos courtesy Lauren Livengood Schaub (left); Susan Morrison (center and right); illustration by Susan Morrison

pp. 162–167: Photos by Virginia Small

p. 168: Photo by Steve Aitken

p. 170: Photo by Melissa Lucas

pp. 171–173: Photos by Steve Aitken

p. 174: Photos by Steve Aitken (right); Virginia Small (left)

p. 175: Photos by Steve Aitken

p. 176–179: Photos © Todd Holloway

p. 180: Photo © Heather Marlow

p. 181: Photo © Todd Holloway

p. 182: Photo © Jerry Pavia

p. 184: Photos © David Cavagnaro (tomato and pepper); courtesy National Garden Bureau, Inc. (basil); by Danielle Sherry (cucumber)

p. 185: Photos by Brandi Spade (thyme); Danielle Sherry (tomato, squash, salad burnett); © Doreen Wynja (blueberry)

p. 186: Photos © Bill Johnson (hosta); © Jerry Pavia (iris)

p. 187: Photos courtesy of Brian Core, Little Valley Wholsesale Nursery (catmint); courtesy Terra Nova Nurseries (coneflower); courtesy Spring Meadow Nursery (roses); © Bill Johnson (spirea); Michelle Gervais (tulip); © Jerry Pavia (haworthia)

p. 188: Photos by Michelle Gervais (sweetflag); © Bill Johnson (prairie dropseed); © Saxon Holt (lovegrass)

p. 189: Photos © Bob Cook (lantana); © Jerry Pavia (pieris); by Jennifer Benner (blue spruce); © Bill Johnson (heather)

p. 190: Photos by Jennifer Benner (magnolia); Steve Aitken (sweetspire); © Bill Johnson (lilac); courtesy of Sandra Reed (hydrangea)

p. 191: Photos © Jerry Pavia (daphne); by Michelle Gervais (cotoneaster); by Melissa Lucas (maple); © Ashley DeLatour (cypress)

INDEX

If you like this book, you'll love *Fine Gardening*.

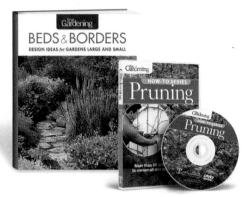